THE MOST BEAUTIFUL ROOMS IN THE WORLD

THE MOST BEAUTIFUL ROOMS IN THE WORLD

A curated selection by the international editors of *Architectural Digest*
edited by Marie Kalt

RIZZOLI NEW YORK

New York · Paris · London · Milan

Certain words come to mind as I page through this book—words like *openness, inclusion, diversity, collaboration.* Yes, the spaces in this volume, chosen by the editors of *Architectural Digest* around the globe, are an escapist delight. They are as elegant, sophisticated, dramatic, and gloriously playful as any rooms you're likely to see. But taken together they suggest to me more than a series of masterworks in the art of interior design. They suggest a powerful new way of looking at the world and how to live in it.

There has been much talk of globalism in our era—it is a word used by politicians and economists and cultural figures in myriad ways. But whatever your perspective, it is undeniable that we live in an age of incredible interconnectedness and movement. National identity is largely what you make of it. Where we feel we come from, who we are, what country we call home—these are ideas that are changing all the time.

And the spaces we live in are extensions of who we are. The rooms in this book, curated from the archives of ten editions of *Architectural Digest,* representing nine countries and the Middle East, remind me that creative influence knows no borders. It is as exhilarating to see Old World glamour in a New York townhouse as it is to perceive the cool currents of American modernism in a chic home in Hangzhou. This is a book of globe-trotting fantasy and romance—you long to be in that book-crowded room in a 1930s house in Shanghai, that wood-paneled study in Eiderstedt, that open-air garden room in Ciudad de México, that lush townhouse on the Place des Vosges.

Indeed these *are* the most beautiful rooms in the world. They burst with color, with art, with maximalist fun, and with ethereal restraint. They bring a sense of intimacy and the familiar, even as they transport us to new places. They remind us of the power of interior design—and leave one feeling optimistic about how much we can learn from each other.

Anna Wintour
Editor-in-Chief, Vogue; *and US Artistic Director and Global Advisor, Condé Nast*

Cover

An old farmhouse facing the Crete Senesi, in Tuscany.
Photo: Massimo Listri

AD
US

A celebration of great
American design
from coast to coast

For the past 100 years, *Architectural Digest* has chronicled the quest for the well-lived life—the life of beauty, inspiration, and comfort. Our search for the world's most spectacular, imaginative homes routinely takes us across the globe, from Manhattan penthouses to Parisian *hôtels particuliers* to the pleasure domes of Bali. But for the first few decades of the magazine's life, *AD* was singularly focused on the glories of California, the magazine's birthplace in 1920.

The young publication elucidated a vision of America's Western frontier as a place of 20th-century innovation and promise, replete with stately Mediterranean-style manses, sun-kissed Italianate gardens, and picturesque reflecting pools. As California became a crucible for the nascent modernist movement in the 1930s and 1940s, the magazine began to revel in the heterogeneity of the California landscape, where New World interpretations of European archetypes mingled amicably with futuristic homes of glass and steel.

Of course, *AD*'s purview expanded long ago beyond the borders of the Golden State. But the spirit and the mission of the magazine remain unchanged. Each month in print, and every day online, we celebrate the myriad wonders of great design. Beyond superficial trends, we delve into the substance of style to spark the imaginations of our readers through glorious images and words. This journey of discovery often takes us to unexpected places, but the surprise makes the adventure all the more fulfilling.

The images we've selected for this volume, mostly drawn from the past decade and limited to projects in the US, present a snapshot of the broad spectrum of American design in the 21st century. Our inheritance from Europe remains an important touchstone. Consider the trompe l'œil—tented room in a San Francisco home by architect G. P. Schafer and designer Miles Redd, which makes a conscious nod to the Casa degli Atellani in Milan; Martyn Lawrence Bullard's lavish décor for Round Hill, a stately manor seemingly transported from the English countryside to Greenwich, Connecticut; and the Mediterranean villa in Montecito, California, that Atelier AM reconceived with a treasure trove of pedigreed Italian and French antiques juxtaposed with major works of modern and contemporary art. All display a reverence for classic Continental style animated with American moxie and imagination. It is, in fact, the melting pot of global references that marks these residences as particularly American in spirit.

The many faces of design in New York City are represented by the luxury of a Park Avenue triplex by designer Michael S. Smith, the alluring bohemian savoir faire of design influencer John Derian's own East Village apartment, and a sublime minimalist aerie by architect John Pawson. Loft living, a quintessentially American innovation, gets a spirited update in the hands of Apparatus founders Gabriel Hendifar and Jeremy Anderson. And for pure avant-garde genius, we've included a jaw-dropping Miami installation by visionary architect Zaha Hadid as well as a giddy, polychromatic, Cali-cool domestic dream by Nikolai Haas of the Haas Brothers.

In these few short pages, there's no way to survey adequately the full range of *AD*'s scope of interest and international influence. But, of course, our own vast home country remains a source of particular pride—and endless inspiration.

Amy Astley
Editor-in-Chief, AD US

New York City

Fashion superstar Marc Jacobs's New York townhouse is a *tour de force* of old-school glamour and serious connoisseurship. Designers Thad Hayes, John Gachot, and Paul Fortune all had a hand in crafting the high-style refuge for Jacobs and his bull terrier, Neville. The blue-chip art collection—including works by John Currin, Cindy Sherman, Richard Prince, and many others—sets the tone.

San Francisco

When a young San Francisco couple asked for old-fashioned, deep-dish decorating, an overjoyed Miles Redd pulled out all the stops. After a renovation by architect Gil Schafer, the 1900s redbrick home's interior received an antiques-heavy redo by Redd. In the entrance hall, the designer invented a tented ceiling in paint, complete with tabs and tassels.

New York City

As this project—his last—proves, the late design legend Mario Buatta retained his masterly vision to the very end. In a glamorous Manhattan duplex for clients with whom he had worked many times, the décor includes the romantic elements essential to Buatta's style. In the marble-clad master bath, the ceiling is covered in a star-spangled Osborne & Little wallpaper.

New York City

Designers Ariel Ashe and Reinaldo Leandro crafted a welcoming home for Ashe's sister and brother-in-law, Alexi and Seth Meyers, in Manhattan's Greenwich Village. Pared-down without being severe, tailored without being uptight, the eight-room duplex is open and bathed in light, featuring bespoke detailing and an attention to craftsmanship.

AD *Volume 76, N°3, March 2019*

New York City

Designers Gabriel Hendifar and Jeremy Anderson of Apparatus transformed a New York City loft into a dazzling showcase of their signature aesthetic. Located on the top floor of an erstwhile industrial building in the Flatiron District, the highly refined and seriously seductive home is filled with prototypes, custom pieces, peculiar *objets de vertu,* and compelling architectural details.

AD *Volume 75, N°9,* October 2018

New York City

Under the masterly guidance of designer Michael S. Smith and architect Oscar Shamamian,
one of Manhattan's most storied residences received a glorious new lease on life. Long considered
one of the city's ultimate trophy apartments, today the eight-bedroom duplex, atop an iconic 1920s
Rosario Candela–designed building, houses a museum-quality collection of art and antiques.

AD Volume 75, N°9, October 2018

New York City

The Manhattan home of John Derian provides a window into the design maestro's world of wonder and beauty. Epitomizing his singular sensibility, Derian brought together timeworn antiques, vintage textiles, and all manner of natural curiosities set alongside pressed-tin ceilings, exposed pipes, and other vestiges of the building's turn-of-the-century roots.

Watch Hill, Rhode Island

Designer Giancarlo Valle rejuvenated a stalwart New England mansion on the coast of Rhode Island for the family of high-flying, high-style entrepreneur Kevin Wendle. Valle paired Wendle's vintage design treasures by the likes of Charlotte Perriand and Le Corbusier with contemporary gems, giving a high-design edge to the traditional residence.

Northern California

Studio Shamshiri and Commune Design worked their subtle magic on a Northern California house
originally decorated by Mark Hampton 30 years ago. Designers Pamela Shamshiri and Roman Alonso
drew inspiration from Italy in the soaring great room, where Renaissance paintings align beneath
a trompe l'œil sky offset by two monumental chandeliers from Mexico.

Northern California

While maintaining this California home's pedigreed bone structure, firms Studio Shamshiri and Commune Design skillfully updated its Old World charm and added contemporary design to the clients' collection of antiques. In a sitting room, olive-green walls act as a foil for a sofa in white linen and a cocktail table and two ottomans upholstered in horsehair.

Rocky Mountains

Architect Peter Marino confidently crafted the ultimate ski getaway for himself and his wife.
Nestled into the slopes, the home features a tapered balcony with a double overhang to take in views
of the stunning landscape. Inside, stone, cedar, and stucco surfaces dominate the minimal décor,
allowing a spectacular art collection to shine.

Miami Beach, Florida

Everyone covets an invitation to the treasure-filled Florida home of real estate magnate and Design Miami founder Craig Robins. Devised by architect Walter Chatham and interior designer Julie Hillman—and boasting a spectacular master bathroom designed by the late Zaha Hadid—the two-story waterfront property in Miami Beach's Sunset Islands is an outlet for Robins's boundless artistic passions.

New York City

Architect John Pawson's seductive Manhattan duplex for the noted antiques dealer Jill Dienst and her family focuses on the poetry of sunlight and shadow. Located just steps from the Hudson River, this home appears blissfully free of visual distractions and is suffused with Pawson's distinctive vocabulary, a signature based on subtle variations of light and exquisite proportions.

Southampton, New York

An A-team of top design talents came together to create a romantic Hamptons escape for one very discerning client. Architect Michael Dwyer, decorating legend Bunny Williams, and landscape architect Quincy Hammond took inspiration from iconic 20th-century manses to craft Mary Ann Tighe's historically inspired, colorful retreat.

AD *Volume 75, N°7, July–August 2018*

Carmel-by-the-Sea, California

On the rugged Carmel coast, designer Jamie Bush reimagined a California landmark as a dazzling home for a young family transplanted from London. Marrying mid-century modern design with contemporary practicality, Bush's indoor-outdoor décor maintains the jewel-box quality of Frank Wynkoop's 1951 Butterfly House for new owners Hannah and Kevin Comolli.

Jackson Hole, Wyoming

Rico and Joanne Zorkendorfer built their young family's dream—long, lean, and environmentally discreet—
on the edge of Wyoming's most famous valley, Jackson Hole. Crafted by London-based architects
McLean Quinlan, the refuge's exterior is clad in honed Montana stone, while the interior features vast
expanses of wood and glass opening to spectacular vistas of the surrounding landscape.

AD Volume 74, N°11, November 2017

Los Angeles, California

Artist Nikolai Haas, half of the Haas Brothers design duo, and stylist Djuna Bel conjured an idiosyncratic wonderland for their family. The layered home, where choice furniture by Haas, Wendell Castle, and others mixes with boho-chic accessories, is made for entertaining, both indoors and out.

Greenwich, Connecticut

Quintessential American fashion designer Tommy Hilfiger and his wife, Dee, transformed a Greenwich, Connecticut, landmark into a home for their family. With a renovation by architect Andre Tchelistcheff and an interior refresh by decorator Martyn Lawrence Bullard, the 1939 manse layers European charms while maintaining its English countryside feel.

AD Volume 74, N°3, March 2017

Montecito, California

Alexandra and Michael Misczynski, the team behind Atelier AM, animated a historic 1930 estate with a contemporary spirit grounded in classic connoisseurship. Deploying reclaimed, handsomely aged wood beams and decking, vintage terra-cotta tile floors, artisanal plaster, Italian marble, and details of gray Pietra Serena sandstone, the residence strikes a lofty Renaissance note.

Los Angeles, California

Designers Nate Berkus and Jeremiah Brent made over a spectacular 1928 Spanish Colonial home for their growing family. Employing a mostly neutral palette, Berkus and Brent relied on texture and patina to animate their personal interiors, juxtaposing rustic wood and stone furnishings with more tailored Continental pieces.

New York City

At Michael Kors's Greenwich Village aerie, the king of jet-set American fashion and his husband, Lance Le Pere, live in high-flying yet down-to-earth style. Wanting to attain a "casual formality," as Kors phrases it, the couple mixed mid-century furnishings with contemporary works, all in a neutral color palette.

AD *Volume 75, N°8, September 2018*

Berkeley, California

For a young Manhattan family recently transplanted to Northern California, the LA design firm
Commune breathed new life into a historic home. With references ranging from Wiener
Werkstätte to Scandinavian design, the updated 1915 redwood home merges unpretentious
bohemian style and a vivid, contemporary spirit.

AD
GERMANY

Bringing color
and intelligent design
to the white cube

2019's Bauhaus centenary reminded us once more that Germany is a land of architects and designers—but perhaps not one of colors and patterns. When Condé Nast launched the German edition of *Architectural Digest* in 1997, the aim was to allow a domestic audience to feast on the world's most beautiful homes and whet its appetite for more. Hitherto, German home interiors magazines, at least of the premium kind, had been the domain of architects, and they invariably choose to emphasize their designs' clean lines via neutral white—understandable but also unoriginal. Interior designers, on the other hand, were, and still are, far less frequently seen in German media. Revealingly, a 2008 obituary of famed decorator Etchika Werner opened with the semi-ironic statement: "Décor is often a catch-all for whatever purists would prefer to banish from home interiors." That may be hogwash, but it tells you something about the context in which we started out.

In the German-speaking world, such attitudes reflect a long and influential tradition spanning architect Adolf Loos's essay "Ornament and Crime" and Braun designer Dieter Rams's dictum of "less but better." There is here a kind of inverse horror vacui at play, with too little décor seen as preferable to too much. This may be rooted in sound intentions and a grain of truth, but, evidently, timidity and rigidity lead to ossification, and that's always been anathema to *Architectural Digest.*

We were, therefore, intrigued by this opportunity to review our own past—to take, as it were, an inward look from outside—and curious to know which interiors would be chosen from our longlist of Germany's finest homes. One thing we can say up front: white cubes didn't stand a chance! Instead, there are light gray cubes, dark gray cubes, concrete cubes, and,

yes, even a black cube. That at least represents progress—after all, the spectrum from palest gray to jet black offers a world of aesthetic possibilities that, for decorators, is fertile ground. Just see for yourself how cool exposed concrete can look when paired with warm textures and intelligent design.

Color, though, has also long since joined the German interiors party. Perhaps surprisingly, even Bauhaus-era modernists experimented with vibrant tones. In Berlin, for instance, the new owners of a 1924 villa by Richard Neutra stripped away old wallpaper to find bold period hues; the kitchen on page 54 is just a warm-up for the fiery red staircase and bedroom in night blue. It was, then, not entirely without precedent when two art dealers chose to give their Frankfurt home salons of red, green, and gray (pages 72 and 73).

Patterns and wall paintings, too, can be found in the featured interiors, though these are not only exceptions to the rule but, invariably, also relics from the past—Delft tiles, say, or baroque Swedish panels. That's a remarkable state of affairs considering that some of the 20th century's most enchanting patterns were penned by Vienna's Josef Frank. Clearly, there's a long way to go before that legacy can be said to live on. On the other hand, without striving for British levels of eccentricity, German interiors can be playful too, as seen in Wolfgang Joop's wonderfully maximalist study or the Münster office carpet based on an antique map.

Oliver Jahn
Editor-in-Chief, AD *Germany*

Chiemgau

For Stephanie Thatenhorst, traditional Bavarian farmhouses seemed too gloomy and cramped. So when her father offered her an unused barn as a country retreat, the Munich-based architect seized the opportunity. Her conversion features exposed roof timbers, gray walls clad in mineral-based plaster, and a fireplace that's no more than a hole in the wall. Spruce stairs lead up to the children's quarters.

AD N°186, February 2018

Berlin

A onetime art student, Sylvester Koziolek realized he was too old-fashioned for the art world. And yet the set designer's home reveals modernist predilections, especially for prewar furniture by the French greats. A Mategot lamp-cum-jardinière and a Pierre Jeanneret *Chandigarh* chair flank a Jean Royère *Ours Polaire* sofa, which Koziolek rejuvenated with lavender plush by Steiff, the stuffed toy company.

AD N°169, May 2016

Berlin

Over the past 20-odd years, Sylvester Koziolek's apartment has seen various phases. Here, the floors and ceiling attest to an earlier black period, as does the tiled kitchen, which boasts pieces by Charlotte Perriand. Today, the dining room is night blue and the picture wall, where Cubism keeps easy company with Truxa's neo-kitsch *Peonies,* is chocolate brown. The low table around the corner is by the French ceramist Roger Capron.

Berlin

Next door to a marine police station, architect Tanja Linke built her family a bungalow on stilts—it sits high above the river, supported by slender pillars and a concrete core. Inside, a zebrano shelf unit serves as a display case and a room divider. The object display and seating were arranged by Linke's husband, the artist Anselm Reyle, while the chandelier once hung in the East German parliament building.

AD N°183, October 2017

Berlin

From its staircase, you might think this 1910 villa was designed not by Emilie Winkelmann, Germany's first female architect, but by M. C. Escher—especially when losing your bearings on its multiple mezzanines. Decorator Etchika Werner further heightened the surreal feel of the place with walls worthy of a spaceship and then, just before Bruno Brunnet and Nicole Hackert (of Contemporary Fine Art) moved in, herself quietly departed this world.

AD N°91, July–August 2008

Berlin

Commissioned by art collector Christian Boros to turn a World War II air-raid shelter into a private museum, Realarchitektur drew up a five-year plan. By the time work was completed, the 2008 crash was unfolding and the new penthouse atop this colossus seemed, with its velvet-and-concrete interiors, like the spartan luxury of tomorrow. Here, an Olafur Eliasson light sculpture watches over a bespoke Zanotta sofa.

Berlin

Just before emigrating to the
US in 1923, Richard Neutra
built a quartet of white cuboid
villas in Zehlendorf that look
Bauhaus through and through.
While renovating theirs,
however, Olin Roenpage and
Penelope Winterhager made
a surprising discovery:
under layers of wallpaper,
they uncovered period colors
ranging from chrome yellow
to arsenic green. The kitchen's
gray, beige, and red scheme
is original, too.

AD N°107, March 2010

Berlin

Sometimes a decorator needs nerves of steel: For the apartment above his gallery, Alfred Kornfeld first decided which of his favorite works should hang where (above, paintings by Neo Rauch and Bruce McLean), and only signed off on the fireplace after rejecting 11 bespoke designs. Gisbert Pöppler persevered, however, and won his Swiss client over with a palette that puts white cubes in the shade.

AD N° 134, November 2012

Munich

After *blitzkrieg* and *ersatz,* at last a positive German loan word: *spritz!* The prosecco and Aperol cocktail's peach-orange hue was exactly what Justin Howlett wanted for his studio apartment. Despite working for property developers Euroboden, the German-American decorator was happy to commit to a rental, even one in unfashionable Sendling, an area where the Aperol spritz is still an alien concept.

Cologne

At media guru Marc Meiré's house, inky black spreads from wall to wall, jumping to the living/dining area's chimney breast, Poliform loungers, and marble-topped Saarinen table. Against this elegantly achromatic backdrop, Florian Baudrexel's wall-hung cardboard sculpture stands out almost as vividly as the study's golden wall.

AD N° 143, October 2013

Münster

The cutesy heroine Princess Lillifee sets alarm bells ringing among progressive parents, but, for publisher
Coppenrath, she's a runaway success. Alarms of a different kind once rang around the firm's HQ,
a converted 1920s fire station. In boss Wolfgang Hölker's office, the interwar harbor scene and map-of-Africa
carpet impress visitors of all ages.

AD N°117, March 2011

Chiemgau

For her barn conversion (see page 46), Stephanie Thatenhorst cut large openings in the façade; one leads
to an outdoor daybed that is the architect's favorite place. Inside, a Flexform sofa, Dimore Gallery designs,
and Gio Ponti *Superleggera* chairs further underscore the urbane look, while the creations that come out
of the kitchen are equally exquisite—the Thatenhorsts run restaurants in Munich.

Eiderstedt

North Sea gales keep the hedges around Peter Nolden's home in check and, although the coast is kilometers away, storm surges are still a recurring event. Thankfully, this 1695 longhouse was built on a mound to protect against flooding, and the interior designer could always take shelter in the period green closet bed on the right. The rustic painted panels come from Sweden.

AD N°163, October 2015

Teltow-Fläming

After stints in Berlin, Cologne, and New York, the gallerist Michael Werner moved to a manor house in Märkisch Wilmersdorf—and thus finally had space for antiques purchased decades before, juxtaposed with works by represented artists such as A. R. Penck and Markus Lüpertz for a gloriously contemporary contrast. Some things, however, can't wait—such as the Delft tiles in this basement nook, which Werner acquired from all over Europe.

AD N°123, October 2011

Munich

When illustrator Jasmin Khezri and family took a top-floor duplex in upscale Bogenhausen, they inherited
not only their predecessor's prayer room, but also a wood-lined salon with two putti over the hearth.
Khezri and interior designer Kirsten Scholz painted the walls Farrow & Ball blue while, for want of a balcony,
the quirky 1950s garden chairs found a home in the living room.

Berlin

In 2011, the couturier Wolfgang Joop was living in a bespoke duplex (by architect Peter Kurz) with a bedroom that resembled a grand tour of Germanic design: the 1889 bed was created and owned by Otto Wagner, later prominent in Viennese art nouveau; the 1929 cactus lamps are by Fritz August Breuhaus de Groot; and the athletes were devised by Otl Aicher, former principal of the Ulm School of Design, for the Olympic Congress of 1981.

AD N°123, October 2011

Munich

Air-raid shelters, part two: developer Stefan Höglmaier gave this Third Reich relic a new civilian existence, converting it into six floors of sophisticated living space. He and his partner, the singer-songwriter Oscar Loya, have kept the upper two and rooftop penthouse for themselves. Today, only impenetrably thick walls and exposed ceilings, as in the dressing room above, attest to the building's military past.

AD N˚163, October 2015

Berlin

Proof Germans don't always shy away from ornament? The prewar apartment above welcomes visitors with chinoiserie motifs showing the continents, while the living room features a hermit in his grotto—two masterful examples of modern-day rococo. "As a child, I wanted to live in a painting, ideally an 18th-century one," says Michael J. Duté, the San Francisco expat behind this walk-in work of art. Ah, so not actually German at all …

Rügen

Rescuing ruined manor houses takes focus and calm, say architect Lars Jakob Hvinden-Haug and artist Tilo Uischner, who also created the inlaid-wood portrait above. Their epic renovation of Gut Udars on the island of Rügen was a constant source of surprises, among them this salon's hand-painted wallpaper fragments. For protection, the pair nailed fly screens over the top—a fairy tale effect.

AD N°193, October 2018

Frankfurt

Based on their five-story townhouse, you might think Michael Neff and husband Philipp Pflug were set designers—but both are art dealers. There's an ice blue kitchen, one salon in matte gray, and another in wall-to-wall green, while the attic's armchairs (Ikea but with new velvet covers) look like part of a site-specific installation, illuminated by Stefan Wieland's cartoonish wall lights.

Frankfurt

Bathed in a raspberry hue, the Red Salon resembles a surrealist lounge: its only furniture is a buttoned four-seater pouf. Designed by owner Michael Neff, this centerpiece would look right at home in a portrait gallery—or a Belle Époque shoe store. Here, it offers views of a Wilhelm Klotzek artwork, Indian string-of-pearl lights, and, thanks to low-level mirrors, the occupants' own feet.

Potsdam

Forced to leave his beloved Bornstedt in the GDR's early years, Wolfgang Joop has now returned to the family estate. As his daughter lives in the villa, the fashion designer converted the old pig house and filled it with fine furniture and art. Eros and Thanatos rule the study from paintings by Ralph Peacock and Richard Müller, while the rococo side table by Otto Wagner's bed (page 66) adds a little Frederician spirit.

AD N°203, October 2019

AD
INDIA

From spare and spiritual
to lush exuberance,
a devotion to craftsmanship

It feels like an exciting time for interior design in India. But the truth is, it always has been. Like in fashion, where India has its own traditional aesthetic and an entire industry of powerful homegrown labels that don't exist in the West, Indian interiors have a long, rich local design language that, frankly, makes fancy Parisian decorators look boring.

Traditional elements of an Indian home, like Gujarati *gaddas* (sofas fashioned from floor cushions that can fit the entire family), *pooja* rooms, and *jali* screens, are, wonderfully, still commonplace and, in the most sophisticated interiors, look modern rather than referential to the past.

Of the two current schools of contemporary interiors in India, the first plays with an evolution of this familiar aesthetic. But rather than hot pink pastiches of Rajasthani palaces, this means joyful pastels, rich print-on-print, and a little bit of an English stately home feel. Let's call it *Indian country house.* The maharaja of this kind of maximalism is Adil Ahmad in Delhi. His theatrical and elegantly considered vignettes make him a favorite of politicians and Bollywood celebrities. And right next to him is the current princess of international interiors, Jaipur-based Marie-Anne Oudejans, whose handful of colorful homes have been so influential they could be described as an entire movement in design. Striped, vaulted ceilings and hand-painted trompe l'œil paneling are her much-copied but never-mastered signatures. Oh, how tempting a tented four-poster can seem, even to a diehard fan of Japanese futons.

The second school of interiors now is cleaner, textured but not embellished, and comes with a spiritual ambience. From Bandra to Goa, the style is almost too ubiquitous: polished concrete floors, modernist chairs from Mumbai's Chor Bazaar, an antique Theyyam head, and a ficus tree. Not quite Axel Vervoordt in India but most definitely *desi wabi sabi*. Most important here is the work of architect Bjioy Jain and Studio Mumbai, whose stone- and teak-built residences whisper of a brilliance that surely makes him a future candidate for the Pritzker Prize. And of the wave of interior decorators who excel at this, most notable is Mumbai-based Ashiesh Shah, who fuses his work with a careful curation of contemporary art, mixed with cult-status international design and craft-focused pieces of his own design.

What unites all significant interiors in India right now is a strong focus on craftsmanship. This is what will define luxury here. The talent in embroidery, stonework, papier mâché, and lacquer is, quite simply, the best in the world, and the reason you can find a roll call of international designers working with Frozen Music in Jaipur, Jean-François Lesage in Chennai, and Maximiliano Modesti in Mumbai. These aren't secrets, but are the obvious names; there is much, much more to be discovered.

The influence of India on global interior design should not be underestimated. Don't forget that the ubiquitous Pierre Jeanneret lounge chairs were born in Chandigarh. A little bit of India found in almost every *AD* home the world over.

Greg Foster
Editor-in-Chief, AD *India*

New Delhi

High ceilings invite light into the villa that entrepreneur Bina Ramani shares
with her daughter Malini, a fashion designer. Throughout, a free-spirited Bohemian
aesthetic reigns. Ramani picked up the antique Shrinathji *pichhwai* in Jaipur.
A Turkish kilim covers a floor in bleached wood.

AD N°26, Volume 5 Issue 1, March–April 2016

New Delhi

Decorated by master maximalist Adil Ahmad, Vasundhara Raje's New Delhi home features a blend of traditional Indian and British colonial styles. In this bedroom, custom-made wallpaper matches a large collection of Daniell aquatints. In the foreground is an antique chessboard inlaid with semiprecious stones, and above it, a hand-carved soapstone light.

Dehradun

In the Himalayan foothills, architect Bijoy Jain and his firm Studio Mumbai built Gangamaki,
a series of buildings that comprise workshops and residences for the Japanese weaver
Chiaki Maki and her team. Maki's private apartment is decorated with Studio Mumbai furniture;
the cushions and upholstery, made of cotton and Tussar silk, were produced in-house.

Alibag

The Palmyra House designed by Bijoy Jain is a magical beachfront estate in the coastal town of Alibag, a ferry ride away from the metropolis of Mumbai. Its two discrete structures in concrete and wood were designed to blur the lines between inside and outside. In the kitchen, the central teak counter has a concrete worktop; above it is a guest room.

Alibag

In the hall of the Palmyra House designed by Bijoy Jain, cement walls and latticed teak contrast with palm trees outside. The wooden structures of this house are built with ain, a local hardwood, using traditional joinery techniques. A low table in Kadappa stone sits in the middle of the open living room; the rush chairs were made on-site by Studio Mumbai.

Mumbai

The work of architect and interior designer Ashiesh Shah, this duplex penthouse in Cuffe Parade, one of Mumbai's most exclusive neighborhoods, is a sprawling home for a family of four. The choice of objects—from tall, sculptural chairs to looming pendant lights and eye-catching artwork—creates a compelling atmosphere in this double-height living room.

New Delhi

Designer Sanjay Garg fashioned a home that reflects his rustic, traditional couture, with earthy colors and natural materials. In the garden, a low sitting area shaded by a bamboo canopy features a table in iron—one of Garg's favorite materials—watched over by a Garuda statue the couturier picked up in Odisha.

AD N°26, Volume 5 Issue 1, March–April 2016

Alibag

Design icon Pinakin Patel's Alibag home reflects his respect for vernacular architecture and his love of tropical modernism. Traditional Gujarati seating designed by Patel occupies the main living area on the lower floor; this room is designed to function as a casual lounge. On the left, a large S. H. Raza painting hangs over works by Zarina Hashmi.

Pune

Kamal and Arjun Malik, the father-and-son duo who are the principal architects at Malik Architecture, chose a spectacular outcrop in the Western Ghats to build their family vacation home. Beneath the natural zinc roof, supported by flinch beams in mild steel and seasoned sal, sits a mix of furniture—*Wassily* chairs, pallet-wood sofas, and a Kerala massage table repurposed as a low table.

New Delhi

The furniture peppered around the home of André Aranha Corrêa do Lago—the Brazilian ambassador to India—
and his wife, Beatrice, reflects the design legacies of global icons. In the sitting room alone, one finds chairs by the
1940s-era Anglo-American architect and designer T. H. Robsjohn-Gibbings, Greek urns dating to the 3rd century BC,
Etruscan and Greek sculptures, and an Oscar Niemeyer drawing above chimney.

New Delhi

An assortment of antique stone sculptures, a painted chest from Sri Lanka, and a rare 17th-century palampore textile make the dining room of designer Vivek Sahni's cottage in the capital a showcase for exceptional vintage pieces. A sleek wooden table and chairs with subtle weaves and spare lines, in black lacquer, dark wood, and cream-colored upholstery, have a stately yet understated presence.

Jaipur

When interior designer Marie-Anne Oudejans took up residence at Jaipur's charming hotel Narain Niwas Palace, she decided to redecorate her suite. The result is luminous and soaring, with canopied daybeds, custom-made Anglo-Indian–style sofas, sultan portraits, and custom-made fabrics.

AD N°40, Volume 7 Issue 1, March–April 2018

Hyderabad

For this home, Rahul Mehrotra and Ashiesh Shah collaborated on the architecture and interior design, respectively. The double-height living room features a long Arper sofa on the right, two *22* armchairs by Jaime Hayon, and the curved Eileen Gray *Monte Carlo* sofa. The hand-knotted wool and silk carpet is from Rugs Refined.

AD N°33, Volume 6 Issue 1, March–April 2017

Chennai

In the living room of this home in the Tamil Nadu state capital, architect Niels Schoenfelder and his entrepreneur wife, Malavika Shivakumar, used Kadappa stone for the floor and indigo-dyed birch for the walls. Adorning the wall are frames containing the complete texts of Johann Wolfgang von Goethe's *Faust* and James Joyce's *Ulysses* in microscopic typeface.

New Delhi

Politician Vasundhara Raje's New Delhi home, designed by Adil Ahmad, blends facets of traditional Indian design and British colonial styling. Taking inspiration from old conservatories, the morning living room features vintage chandeliers, bamboo-patterned wallpaper, and a full-length portrait of the homeowner's grandfather-in-law, Maharaja Rana Udaibhan Singh of Dholpur.

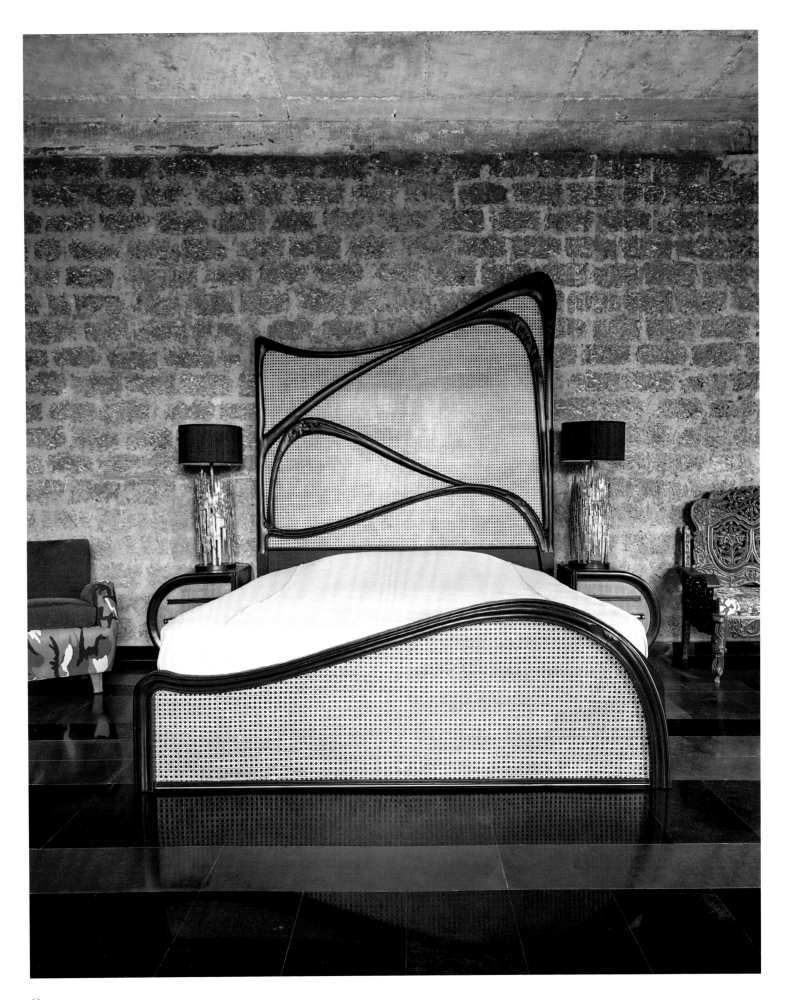

Goa

Known as much for its party beaches as its relaxed, *susegad* (from the Portuguese *sossegado*, meaning quiet) atmosphere, Goa is where designer Vikram Goyal built his holiday home, with the help of local architect Tallulah D'Silva. The laterite structure—which also features Kadappa and Macherla stone and concrete— is home to many pieces of furniture and décor from Viya Home, Goyal's design brand.

Kolkata

A grand old mansion is home
to the king of Indian fashion,
Sabyasachi Mukherjee.
A Portuguese mirror forms
the focal point, and wooden
pelmets are topped with a mix
of antiques and bric-a-brac,
Chinese ginger jars, and Dutch
pottery. Plantation sofas are
upholstered in fabrics like
Bangladeshi *nakshi kantha*
and Varanasi brocade, all set
within a vintage jade room,
a Sabyasachi signature.

*AD N°43, Volume 7 Issue 4,
September 2018*

New Delhi

Fashion designer Tarun Tahiliani decorated his home with his own eclectic collection. The dining room, which overlooks the swimming pool and garden, features reproduction Irani café chairs at a circular dining table decorated with ostrich eggs from South Africa, set around traditional metalwork from Zanzibar. Large shells from the Andaman Islands serve as salad plates.

AD N°37, Volume 6 Issue 5, October 2017

New Delhi

Veteran ad man V Sunil's home, designed by Saurabh Dakshini, is warm yet modern, a reflection of his contemporary aesthetic and traditional elements from his home state of Kerala. The guest rooms on the first floor feature en suite baths that open onto private outdoor shower areas. Most rooms in the house are, like this one, generously fitted with built-in storage.

Mumbai

In the chic Juhu suburb of Mumbai, Sanjay and Ina Arora—whose family runs fabric giant D'Decor—
tasked the Argentina-born, Singapore-based architect Ernesto Bedmar with designing their home.
Vast windows in the double-height living room let natural light stream in and offer sweeping views of
the garden and pool. All the furniture is by Christian Liaigre. The red centerpiece bowl is from Roche Bobois.

Alibag

The sand-covered floor sets the tone at architect Nozer Wadia's beachside home. An imposing 18-foot sofa crafted in solid mahogany looks out toward a postcard-perfect view of the sea. The sofa and armchairs are from Mumbai's Chor Bazaar and were restored by Mahendra Doshi, an antiques store in the city. The cushions are from Jim Thompson in Thailand.

AD N°40, Volume 7 Issue 1, March–April 2018

Puducherry

A spectacular 19th-century mansion is home to the embroiderer Jean-François Lesage. The first-floor salon is lit by a crystal chandelier—restored by Mathieu Lusterie—dating to the 1860s, which Lesage transported from his family home near Versailles. The "tiger skin" rug and armchair upholstery were embroidered at Vastrakala. The polished cement tile floor is original to the house.

AD
FRANCE

Telling a story
of elegance in
fine-tuned mixes

Even after so many years working in the world of interior design, I find it as difficult as ever to define the French style. Harmony, elegance, refinement... These are the words that leap to mind, resonating with the great eras in the history of decoration. From the splendor of the 18th century to the modernist innovations of the 1930s and the revolution of the 1960s and 1970s, certain elements remain unchanged: a taste for balance, precision of line, the beauty of the forms. Clearly nurtured by these influences, the interior designers of today have assimilated this heritage, making it a template with which to create spaces that update the tenets of classicism in well-proportioned volumes and a tendency toward symmetry. Each of their projects is a blank canvas waiting to be enriched with a palette of colors, materials, textures, and embellishments.

On this topic, it must be admitted that the use of color is not always their forte. Aside from a few free spirits like India Mahdavi, Luis Laplace, and more recently Pierre Yovanovitch, who wield it with talent and *élan,* many French designers seem to prefer subtle monochromes of whites and beige tones. But this "chromatic reticence" is counterbalanced by the infinite array of materials offered by France's plasterers, bronzesmiths, cabinetmakers, and other specialists in the use of stone, glass, painted effects... These artisans, whose know-how and techniques are admired around the world, are the cherished partners of every creator of décors. Producing coffered ceilings, door handles, marble bathtubs, velvet sofas, or bronze tables for the ever-greater number of interior designers who create custom furniture for their clients, these craftsmen make it possible to conceive each space as a unified whole, echoing another grand French tradition: that of the *ensemblier* decorators of the early 20th century.

It is by juggling and coordinating all of these components that the designers, deploying their own tastes and skills, compose their décors. Above all, it's about telling a story, instilling an atmosphere by combining personal creations with vintage furniture, contemporary artworks with erudite references. Some, like François-Joseph Graf, allude to history, while others, like Jacques Garcia, reinvent it. Then there are those who, like Vincent Darré, subvert it, giving it a surrealist twist, or, like Jacques Grange, take pleasure in mixing it up. The iconic furniture designers of the 20th century are often called into play: Carlo Scarpa and Gio Ponti for Charles Zana, Charlotte Perriand and Pierre Jeanneret for Joseph Dirand, Paul Evans and Harry Bertoia for Chahan Minassian. But they are just one element in a complex composition of nuances based on the art of juxtaposition. Indeed, beyond its anchoring in a decorative heritage, what characterizes the French style of today is this flair for blending styles and periods, this sense of the "perfect mix," along with that ineffable quality that makes it unique and immediately recognizable: true chic.

Marie Kalt
Editor-in-Chief, AD *France*

Paris

For the décor of his apartment, interior designer Jacques Grange sought to perpetuate the spirit of the property's former owner, the French author Colette (1873–1954). Many original elements have been preserved while others are entirely new, like the sculptural spiral staircase that dominates the entryway, designed by Grange and inspired by Man Ray's lampshade.

AD100 Special Interior Design Issue, 2020

Paris

In Colette's former apartment, Jacques Grange has kept the living room nearly as it was. Alongside keepsakes that belonged to the author, some of them gifts from her neighbor, Jean Cocteau, the interior designer has added a painting by Robert Motherwell (at top), an abstract canvas by Carla Accardi, and a graceful chair facing the window overlooking the Comédie-Française.

Paris

Fabrizio Casiraghi contributed this erudite living room to a project for which *AD* France offered young talents carte blanche to create a décor. The Milanese interior designer based in Paris took a mix-and-match approach, blending Italian furniture with Moroccan craftsmanship, Chinese antiques, and two of his own pieces, a sofa and a lacquered coffee table, specially made for the occasion.

AD N° 145,
December 2017–January 2018

Paris

The light-filled entryway of the apartment designed by architect Luis Laplace for the top model
Adriana Abascal Schreder was inspired by a shared devotion to contemporary art, with a neon
work by Pae White, a canvas by Christopher Wool, and a Carl Andre floor sculpture. Laplace's décor
strikes an ideal balance between the classic lines of the space and the owner's art collection.

AD N°137, August–September 2016

Méribel

In the famous Alpine ski resort, designer Noé Duchaufour-Lawrance transformed a mountain refuge into a quasi-futuristic living space. The owners wanted a contemporary interior highlighting regional materials, especially wood and stone. An approach exemplified in this living room, with its sculptural fireplace and elegant array of furniture, including pieces by the designer himself.

Paris

For his family's loft in Montmartre, interior designer Tristan Auer concocted an adventuresome mix of vintage references, art nouveau, and his own creations. In the master bedroom, a copper and sycamore headboard dialogues with statues by the French sculptor Gérard Choain, who was best known for monumental and funerary works.

AD N°143, August–September 2017

Paris

Three friends collaborated on the décor in what was once the office of Elsa Schiaparelli, the legendary surrealist couturiere of the interwar period: interior designer Vincent Darré, who contributed the colorfully patterned rugs; author Francis Dorléans; and the illustrator Pierre Le-Tan, who dreamed up the column-framed bookcases. A highly personal, exuberant vision of neoclassical style.

AD N°115, April 2013

French Vexin Regional Natural Park

Interior designer Jacques Garcia restored the splendid 17th-century Château de Villette to its former glory. One of the former bedrooms is now a sumptuous bathroom: on the marble floor, an onyx bathtub that belonged to the celebrated courtesan La Païva is surrounded by lacquered and mirrored panels, a Louis XIV–era torchère, a hanging lantern, and 18th-century gilded bronze sconces.

Paris

For the living room of this apartment, whose distinctive features include an unobstructed view of the Eiffel Tower, interior designer Joseph Dirand centered the décor on a marble coffee table of his own design. Surrounding it are a desk by Pierre Chareau, sofas and a chauffeuse by Pierre Jeanneret, plus a cube by Le Corbusier, beneath a chandelier by Philippe Anthonioz. Replacing the conventional mirror over the fireplace, a painting by Angel Alonso resonates with a work by Elliot Dubail, at left.

AD N°160, May–June 2020

Paris

Describing his apartment, the interior designer Chahan Minassian says, "It represents the quintessence of my style and my finest showcase." A champion of strikingly original furniture designs, Minassian was one of the first in Paris to show pieces by the brutalist designer Paul Evans, like this bronze resin over wood cabinet from 1969, placed under a photograph by the American artist Jack Pierson.

AD N°131, August–September 2015

Paris

Interior designer Chahan Minassian decorated the long entrance hall of his apartment in a palette of ivory tones, punctuated with solid black accents and a selection of objects and artwork that enlivens the space, such as a mural by David Roth, an Ettore Sottsass seat, and a lion by Olivier Strebelle. An approach that puts the emphasis on shapes and materials.

French Riviera

Interior designer India Mahdavi composed a medley of optical and ultra-graphic effects for this Mediterranean house owned by the art dealer Jean-Gabriel Mitterrand and his son Edward. Serving as a private exhibition space, the property is surrounded by a contemporary sculpture park, visible through the glassed-in arches giving onto the veranda.

AD N°151,
November–December 2018

Paris

At home with Carlos Couturier, founder of the Grupo Habita boutique hotels collection. For his home office, he asked the architects at Lecoadic-Scotto to create a Parisian-chic space tinged with a Bauhaus spirit, which comes through in the ceiling lamp, a modular table custom-made by the design agency, and a bookcase with glassed-in display niches that lend the room structure.

AD N°148, May–June 2018

Paris

For the 2013 edition of the *AD Intérieurs* exhibition, the architect and designer Charles Zana dreamed up
a space conceived as a living room that opens onto a kitchen—and not vice versa. An outsized sofa
of his own design structures the space, while soft light filters through linen curtains with a tie-dye effect.
A temporary décor as carefully crafted as that of a private residence.

AD Intérieurs exhibition, 2013

Paris

Gilles & Boissier, the studio headed by interior designers Dorothée Boissier and Patrick Gilles, composed the décor of this classic 19th-century Parisian apartment, with gilded moldings extending from the floor to the high ceiling. Under a Bohemian crystal chandelier found at a Paris flea market, a selection of furniture, lamps, sculptures, and other objects from Gilles & Boissier's collection *Les Choses* gives the living room a contemporary feel. On the wall to the left is a painting by Christian Astuguevieille, and on the right, a work by the artist Joseph Hoffmann.

AD N°162,
September–October 2020

Toulouse

For this 18th-century townhouse, interior designers Daniel Suduca and Thierry Mérillou composed
an imaginative blend of neoclassical furniture and contemporary artworks. The centerpiece
of the dining room is a pop-style table by the artist-chemist Louis Durot. The chairs by Maison Jansen
are found in various rooms, recalling the previous, 1960s-era décor by the historic design firm.

AD N°150, September–October 2018

Paris

Interior designer Caroline Sarkozy worked closely with the antiques specialist Jacques Lacoste on the décor of this apartment in the Madeleine district. The result combines her cosmopolitan taste and penchant for Nordic design with his expertise in French modernist pieces from the postwar period. The fireplace seen here is crafted from glass, metal, and ceramic.

The Alps

Interior designer Pierre Yovanovitch captured the spirit of the Alps in a décor featuring wool and wood for a duplex atop a building in a ski resort. A double half-circle bench, made to measure by the cabinetmaker Pierre-Éloi Bris, is ensconced under an installation of 11 faceted pendant lamps by the pop-oriented artist Jeff Zimmermann.

AD N°133, December 2015–January 2016

The Alps

The living room of the duplex by Pierre Yovanovitch commands a sweeping view of the valley
and the mountain village. The entire floor is conceived as a cozy cocoon, with comfortable furniture
like asymmetrical armchairs by Yovanovitch and coffee tables by Matthias Kohn, plus screening
on the balcony railing and windows to soften the light. A striking update on Alpine lifestyle.

Paris

The owner of this apartment asked Karl Fournier and Olivier Marty of Studio KO to give the interiors fresh energy. The dining room contrasts precious surfaces, like rosewood parquet and a brass screen, with more artisanal materials, like a wicker armchair and vintage ceramic bowl. At right, behind the partition, the apartment's entrance is paneled entirely with mirrors.

AD N°150,
September–October 2018

Paris

With a magnificent décor orchestrated by François-Joseph Graf, the apartment of businessman Pierre Bergé
was a trove of unique treasures. For this devoted bibliophile, the interior designer transformed the library
into a spectacular showcase. Above the sofa, a resplendent portrait by the 17th-century artist Cornelis de Vos
is framed by Limoges enamels against a wall lined with Cordoba leather.

AD N°81, February–March 2009

Paris

From the vestibule of Pierre Bergé's apartment, a double door leads to the dining room, decorated with chinoiseries and paintings dating from the Enlightenment. All of these rare gems were sold separately in an auction at Christie's after the death of Bergé's longtime partner, Yves Saint Laurent. A grandiose interior that illustrated François-Joseph Graf's flair for creating cultivated décors.

s lively imagination free rein, a Parisian collector brought together tribal art, art nouveau, and
niture to create this opulent décor for a townhouse on the Place des Vosges. A painting by
Le Sueur and a monumental 17ᵗʰ-century tapestry from Bruges are juxtaposed with a metal buffet
ise See and chairs by Warren Platner, creating an unexpected and striking visual harmony.

AD
RUSSIA

Homegrown taste
nurtured by a
cosmopolitan spirit

Over the course of the 20th century, Russia shifted realities multiple times: more than once, its people literally woke up to a changed country. Compared to historical and economic shifts, interior design may not seem all that significant—and yet what is concealed behind the doors of private homes and apartments reveals much more about current events than official headlines do. Someday, sociologists may find this magazine a highly informative source. But for the time being, I can note—with some surprise—that the interiors we covered 10 or 15 years ago look just as interesting and current now as they did then.

In the late 1990s, there was only one architecture school in Moscow and the profession of decorator, as we know it today, was nonexistent. Not very propitious conditions for establishing local interior design traditions. But the quest for beauty, and the innate curiosity, enthusiasm, and talent of those who entered this sphere (and from the most unexpected places) triumphed. The top Russian designers come from all walks of life: they may be former financiers or marketing experts, lawyers or doctors. At some point, each took a risk and made a radical change—and as a result transformed how we live.

In Russia there have been times when there wasn't enough money or freedom (or both) but—perhaps surprisingly, for some—there was never a dearth of good taste. When the first edition of *AD* Russia came out in 2002, those people were its protagonists. In the early years, the magazine offered not so much an objective view of Russian interiors, but rather provided benchmarks: what to aspire to, whose cues to follow. Now, looking over interiors from the past five years, I am grateful to my predecessors, Karina Dobrotvorskaya and Yevgeniya Mikulina, who spearheaded this effort. At the same time, I delight in the designers and clients who absorbed our lessons so flawlessly.

Russian architects and decorators mastered the art of interior design as "externs." They didn't have legends like Dorothy Draper, Frank Lloyd Wright, Madeleine Castaing, and John Lautner to learn from. Neither did their clients have any role models other than those they spotted in magazines during their travels. But that weakness transformed into a strength. It's easy for us to slip into other decorative cultures: we are inspired by Parisian apartments, we love the scale of classical American homes, we prize the coziness of English-style interiors. We may dream of an Alpine chalet, but we also honor our own country cottage traditions and select plots of land with complex topography in order to build a home in the pure modernist tradition. When it comes to private architecture and design, Russians are truly cosmopolitan.

The first generation of Russian interior design clients took their projects to heart and plunged headfirst into an extraordinary experience. They learned about architectural styles as they went along, absorbed the heritage of legendary 20th-century designers, and studied in order to appreciate antiques and fine craftsmanship. Over time, a thirst for personal involvement—in an equal partnership with the designer—has been replaced by trust in professionalism. If I had to choose one word for what happened to Russian design these past few decades, I'd say it has matured.

It's much trickier to sum up what's so special about contemporary Russian style. As we all know, Russians abroad are considered true *bon vivants*—carriers of a perennial luxury gene and lovers of Byzantine excess. Even so, opulence is not the dominant currency in contemporary Russian interiors; it coexists equally with a desire for minimalism. They are also more eclectic and varied than anyone might suspect—and, clearly, gold plating is no longer a measure of quality in furniture and rooms. Indeed, if there is a common thread in these pages, it is a wish to choose the best the world has to offer and make it one's own. If you ask me, it doesn't get more Russian than that.

Anastasia Romashkevich
Editor-in-Chief, AD *Russia*

Moscow

Art expert Katya Gulyuk transformed a house in Kratovo, near Moscow, into a space "for a quiet life." Everything centers around a living/dining area decorated with 19th-century furniture and angels by the Belorussian artist Natalya Pinevich. A Swedish-style fireplace features artisanal tiles from Gzhel, while the frescoes in the staircase were inspired by Alpine interiors.

AD N°163, July 2017

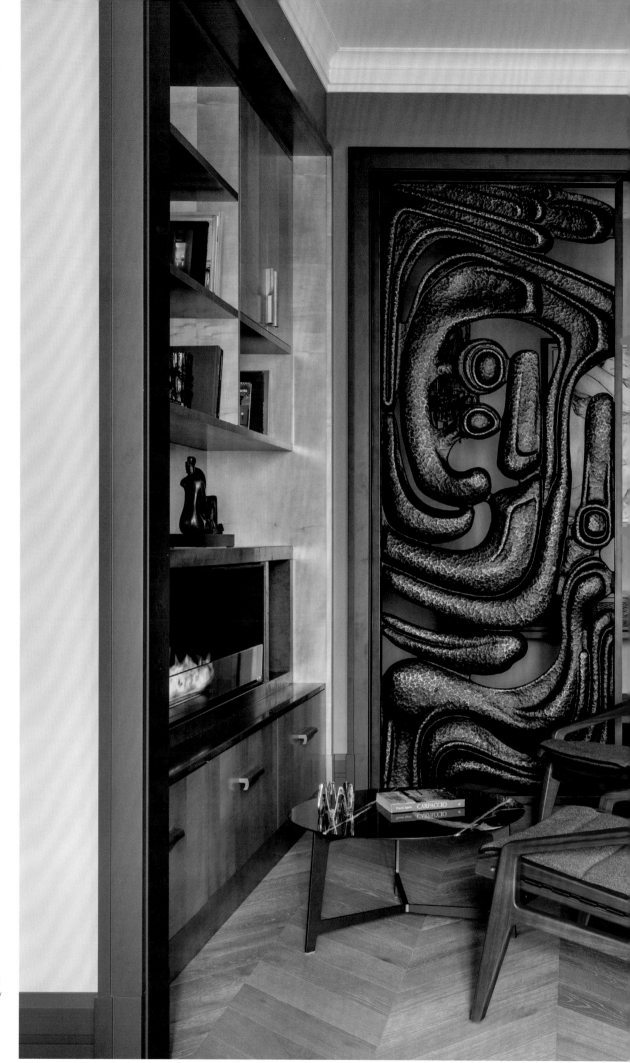

Moscow

In an apartment on Moscow's Patriarch's Ponds—a setting made famous in Bulgakov's *The Master and Margarita*—Nadezhda Ananeva and her partner (and husband) Georgy came up with a color scheme in shades of gray and mimosa as the backdrop for an eclectic assortment of vintage furniture, contemporary re-editions of iconic mid-century designs, and art sourced at local art fairs and galleries.

AD *Special Issue, The Best Designers in Russia, 2019*

Moscow

A master of sumptuous classical interiors, Kirill Istomin gave an outdated 1990s-era suburban home a vibrant new lease on life. Working closely with the owner—health food entrepreneur Darya Lisichenko, whose parents built the house—Istomin sidestepped radical change and opted instead for an eclectic mix of family heirlooms, custom-made furniture, and antiques found at auction.

AD N°182, April 2019

Moscow

The architect Nikolai Belousov works at the intersection of typical Russian wooden architecture and contemporary design. "Sun Trap," as his home outside Moscow is known, is built of traditionally felled logs yet features lots of glass, which allows natural light to flood the house throughout the day. Contemporary furniture and an avant-garde fireplace look like natural extensions of the architecture.

Moscow

For clients who had long dreamed of building an Alpine-style chalet in the forest outside Moscow, Sergey Kolchin and Nadezhda Torshina of Le Atelier helped realize an even more compelling design. A complex floor plan takes into account land elevation, counterbalanced by a monastic interior. The couple also designed most of the furniture, including an imposing wooden bed.

AD *Special Issue, Top 100 Designers and Architects in Russia, 2018*

Saint Petersburg

Rubinshtein Street in Saint Petersburg is known for its lively food and bar scene, so decorators Polina Gerasimova and Svetlana Kalimanova of Ruger Design, along with their client, decided to dispense with a fully functional kitchen. Instead, they fitted the essentials into a brass cube near the entrance. Whenever the owner, a music lover, decides to entertain, this feature converts into a buffet table.

AD *Special Issue, Top 100 Designers and Architects in Russia, 2018*

Moscow

This penthouse atop the "City of Yachts" does not just overlook the Moscow Canal—it actually seems to hover above the water. Designer Olga Surkova made the surroundings the focal point, arranging furniture to optimize the view. Reflecting the owners' love of natural materials, the interior décor centers on pieces in noble woods, complemented by custom-made leather sofas.

AD *Special Issue, Top 100 Designers and Architects in Russia, 2017*

Moscow

Rarely do Darya Kasatskaya and Filip Tangalychev of Studioplan agree to finish a project started by another team, but they made an exception for the owners of a 140-square-meter apartment in a new building in Moscow. They "fine-tuned" by adjusting the layout, adding built-in shelves in the hall, and structuring the décor with cement elements and classics of contemporary design.

Moscow

A two-story apartment in an old Moscow building offered a challenge for its new owners, whose treasure came with a pretentious 1990s-era décor. Decorator Olimpiada Arefyeva updated the space without heavy renovations thanks to a judicious selection of color, fabric, and wallpaper. Now in bold yellow, the spacious living room features classical carpets, floral fabrics, and fine art.

AD N°152, July 2016

Moscow

For this apartment in a historic
Moscow building, designers
Elena Solovyeva and Ilya Klimov
of Art-Bureau 1/1 left the interior intact and updated its spirit
with contemporary designer
furniture. A gypsum décor and
a collection of paintings by
mid-century Russian artists
create a feeling of authenticity,
complemented by custom
painted façades by the artist
Yekaterina Rozhkova in
the kitchen.

AD N°160, April 2017

Moscow

For an apartment in the new Legends of Tsvetnoy high-rise, the architects Lydia, Zlatan, and Vedran Brkich of Ab-architects worked in concert to meet the owners' desire for an interior with literal polish, in natural stone and glass. In the master bath, marble walls mirror the metal-framed door as well as the picture windows in the adjacent bedroom.

AD N°160, April 2017

Moscow

This Moscow apartment overlooking Gregory Neokesariysky cathedral has remained in the same family for three generations. Today, it is home to designer Yekaterina Nechaeva, cofounder of the studio BHD, who furnished it with lovingly restored heirlooms and other archival mementos. Updated elements include new flooring and a bold, vibrant color palette inspired by the cathedral itself.

Moscow

Decorator Irakli Zaria designed this apartment for a young design-savvy client who had spent nearly half her life in England. A monochrome interior evokes a bygone era and belies a complex color palette that is actually devoid of pure white. Vintage furniture from the owner's family collection keeps company with custom-made elements such as a sofa and a parchment fire screen designed by Zaria.

AD N°184, June 2019

Tarusa

Ever popular among bohemians, the old city of Tarusa is now home to the Melik-Pashaevy publishing family. Having purchased a house, the owners decided to expand and called on Alexei Dunaev of PROEKT905 to transform a traditional cottage into a visually concise, contemporary residence. A minimalist baseline acts as a foil for antiques like dining room chairs and an "aristocratic rustic" sideboard.

AD N˚179, December 2018–January 2019

Moscow

This house in the green district of Moscow belongs to a lover of all things art nouveau, from objects and furniture to fashion. The search for a designer who could interpret a turn-of-the-century collection harmoniously in an interior—despite all the inherent challenges—led her to Maria Biryukova, who rose to the occasion with an aesthetic that perfectly reflects the owner's personal style.

Moscow

For this Gothic-influenced home near Moscow, Art-Bureau 1/1 created an interior to accommodate the owner's personal art collection while honoring the house's unusual façade. Historical allusions punctuate a contemporary space: In a room with high, vaulted ceilings, a French fireplace and an 18th-century chair sit alongside the late 19th-century painting *Girl with Grapes* by Alexey Kharlamov.

Moscow

Having worked with designer Gulya Galeeva on his Moscow home more than 15 years ago, collector
Oleg Baibakov called on her again when he decided to furnish his home outside Moscow. Though
the starting point was the owner's personal art collection, Galeeva knew that those pieces would be on
frequent rotation, so she created a space in which the only thing that changes is what's on the walls.

AD N°177, October 2018

Moscow

Decorator Leila Ulukhanli worked closely with feng shui experts to realize this apartment in a contemporary classic style with elements of art deco. In lieu of bright colors, brass and gold illuminate the décor, notably through an imposing and elegant chandelier in the living room. As Ulukhanli also designs furniture, she custom-made a commode with selenite surfaces specifically for this space.

AD Special Issue, Top 100 Designers and Architects in Russia, 2017

Moscow

To achieve authentic, French-style interiors, decorator Natela Mankaeva looks to Alberto Pinto and Jacques Garcia. For this home outside Moscow, Mankaeva eventually convinced the owners that their wish for classical period décor called for saturated colors. In the living room, contemporary replicas of classic furniture keep company with paintings by Ruslan Setsky and Anton Antonov.

AD *Special Issue, Top 100 Designers and Architects in Russia, 2018*

AD
SPAIN

Ever-evolving creativity
founded on rich
historical crosscurrents

In the history of Spanish décor, most of the action takes place not in what glitters, but in the shadows. Under Felipe II, the 16th-century heir to the throne, the sun never set on the Spanish Empire. Even so, in the palaces of Spanish nobility and the houses of illustrious intellectuals like Lope de Vega, treasures from America barely glimmered. A conventual, Spartan aesthetic reigned, with whitewashed walls, dark woods, tin jugs, and heavy velvet curtains with trim. As if lifted from a tenebrist still life by the 17th-century artist Francisco de Zurbarán, severity blurred with chiaroscuro, adapting over the years to outside tastes and influences even as the inherent decorative language remained constant.

Of course, unique voices emerged, among them Mariano Fortuny and his 19th-century silk lamps, the painter Josep Maria Sert, who decorated villas in the 1930s, and the architect Javier Carvajal, who championed rationalism during Franco's regime. Finally, in the 1980s— and all the more so with the 1992 Olympic Games—Barcelona disseny dictated how hotels and restaurants should look (in Spain and around the world). Meanwhile, at home, we mainly continued adopting foreign styles, from Provençal to Gustavian, British to French.

In the 21st century, Spain follows its own path. We're once again proud of our heritage; local designers create innovative mixes in pure spaces and even dare to appropriate old Castilian furniture and the tradition of the Spanish Golden Age. The timeless, native values of functionality, simplicity, and honest use of materials have regained currency. Rather than faithfully reproducing tradition, today's aesthetic offers a more humane, truthful view of living spaces, with rough stucco, unplastered brick, clay tiles, and wooden beams that look as contemporary as resin or cut steel. In a country rich with Roman and Arabic influences, vernacular architecture, artisanal finishes, and popular techniques inspire anew.

AD Spain aptly reflects this creative spirit. Launched in 2006, the magazine aimed to take an untapped gold mine and shake up Spanish interior design, show what was happening both inside and out, and inspire change. We love audacity, color, escape from monotony, and discovering new ways of living and enjoying the home environment. In our pages, we encourage unconventional mixes and the shedding of timidity or preconceived notions: designers incorporate Ikea, vintage embraces antiques, contemporary art dallies with Ming vases, classic painting converses with radical photography, and delicate pieces flirt with the raw, pure Spanish spirit, accentuated by the glint of brass and artisanal esparto.

At AD Spain, we are bold, modern, surprising, daring, and open to all suggestions. The magazine's editorial line is a joyful fusion of irreverence, Mediterranean style, contemporary art, the finest 20th-century vintage, splendid bohemia, exquisite prints, simple luxuries, contemporary design, and nuanced white with color. We draw the line at immobility, instant décor concepts that never budge, and the stasis of furnishing and upholstering for a lifetime. We see homes as a creative lab: fun, living beings that grow and evolve, develop and change along with their inhabitants—us.

Enric Pastor
Editor-in-Chief, AD *Spain*

Barcelona

A sophisticated tribute to the Mediterranean, the apartment of Gabriel Escámez from Cobalto Studio creates a rationalist, artisanal, and rough vernacular in concrete, lime, brick, ceramic, and tiles. In the living room, a sofa in Dedar fabric finds a rough-hewn counterpoint in a naga wood table by Azul Tierra, a sleek rocking chair in wood and leather, artisanally crafted stools, and a painting discovered at a local flea market.

AD N° 144, March 2019

Madrid

The owner, a contemporary art collector, asked architect and interior designer Jean Porsche to make art the focal point of this stately apartment in downtown Madrid. The result is a baroque-minimalist style that incorporates large art installations, chandeliers, tapestries, and art deco furniture. A metal curtain by Daniel Steegman Mangrané divides the hall, and a Miriam Cahn oil painting hangs over a fireplace also designed by Porsche.

AD N°143, February 2019

Madrid

In the living room, Jean Porsche drew on colors in a monumental work by Secundino Hernández to blend contemporary and classic: a blue velvet sofa by Coordonné anchors an eclectic mix that includes an armchair in a William Morris print, a rug with a classic motif by La Real Fábrica de Tapices, and modern coffee tables from The Interiorlist decorated with a Neapolitan ceramic head and a Brian Rochefort vase.

Matarraña, Aragón

Near the mountains of Lower Aragón, developer Christian Bourdais and art producer Eva Albarrán,
as part of the Solo Houses project, built a concrete ring opening onto the forest, designed
by Office KGDVS. Around the perimeter, polycarbonate and galvanized steel panels allow rooms
to be open or enclosed. An interior garden reinforces the impression of blending into the landscape.

AD N° 126, July–August 2017

the most
important things
are not
things

Madrid

Designer and journalist Jesús Cano chose a warm, modern-eclectic atmosphere for his 85-square-meter penthouse, with *Wood Grain* wallpaper by Tortoise General Store, a 1930 cabinet by Tiempos Modernos, a *Déjà-vu* chair by Naoto Fukasawa, a *Barcelona* daybed by Mies van der Rohe, a Noguchi coffee table by Vitra, Ester Partegàs's *The most important things are not things* on framed toile de Jouy, and a Moroccan rug.

AD N°76, January 2013

Madrid

Decorator Pepe Leal lives in a 90-square-meter penthouse. "You can tell that I'm getting old because the house is more relaxed and has more weight to it," he notes. Here, a brass door gives onto the bedroom. On the walls, a Marset *Funiculí* light mingles with a 1920s Moroccan coffee table; velvet bedspread by Güell-Lamadrid, embroidered petit point and Hungarian cushions from the 1940s.

Oropesa, Toledo

Designer Marta de la Rica transformed an old farmhouse into an impressive country home surrounded by expansive grounds dedicated to *El Milagro* sustainable agriculture. With the help of local artisans, traditional elements were repurposed for modern times, creating a warm, friendly interior. Here, a table made from parquet flooring, vintage chairs, and a 19th-century gate contrast with *Pet Lamps* by Álvaro Catalán de Ocón.

AD N°144, March 2019

Madrid

An architect with artistic leanings, Amaro Sánchez de Moya keeps to a neoclassical style for his clients,
but chose to recreate a perfect past in his own flat. A lover of all things 18th century, he brought
Piranesi engravings, Grand Tour souvenirs, and rich textiles together in every room. An orange and black
half-bath features an antique sink, a French nude painting, and erotic prints from Pompeii.

AD N°123, April 2017

Barcelona

Radical designer Guillermo Santomà lives in a labyrinthine 19th-century house. In lieu of décor, he chose optical effects and symmetry, with color and some iconic furniture by Mackintosh, Castiglioni, Botta, and De Lucchi. A soft pink dining room features graffiti by Maria Pratts and, around a large table, an array of painted plastic garden chairs, which Santomà previously burned.

Madrid

Texture, natural tones, and great design come together in architect Iker Ochotorena's apartment, with austere bleached oak and bone-colored lime walls devoid of skirting boards. A 1970s table by Willy Rizzo, a B&B Collection sofa, Jeanneret's *Chandigarh* daybed, a Perriand stool, Daphine *Terra* lamps by Tommaso Cimini, and silk carpet by Rica Basagoiti. At left, Fritz Hansen armchairs and an Ado Chale side table.

AD N°150, October 2019

Madrid

Decorator Lorenzo Castillo lives in a 1,000-square-meter palace in the heart of the Spanish capital that was previously a costume store—and, before that, a 17th-century convent and the 18th-century home of a count. The dining room is designed like a bistro, with glass and brass tables by Castillo and a banquette found in a New York warehouse. Ralph Lauren Home wallpaper, 1970s yellow cubes by Iturralde, and Vasarely geometries.

AD N°35, April 2009

Madrid

In Luis Bustamante's house, Spanish contemporary art and antiques mix with furniture of his own design in a predominantly black and white palette. In a corner of the large library, a Roman-inspired white marble bathtub by Bustamante, manufactured by José Antonio Couso, sits below an oil painting by José Guerrero, flanked by two marble sculptures bought in Paris.

Empordà, Girona

Interior designer Serge Castella transformed a 1970s villa in Empordà into a neutral box where humble materials coexist with design treasures. In the living room, a *Jacqueline* sofa by Castella, upholstered in *Esparto* cotton for Gancedo, a Roger Capron table, *Romeo & Juliet* armchairs by Guillerme et Chambron, bamboo stools by Gabriella Crespi, and an *Almeria* rug by Castella. Original fireplace, surmounted by a William Bowie sculpture.

AD N°108, December 2015

Palma de Mallorca

With high-energy colors, a touch of pop, daring, and humor, architect Teresa Sapey transformed a 19th-century palace into a summer house with a contemporary take on the Mediterranean spirit. On the wall, a color-blocked mural in sunny yellow and sea-and-sky blues takes a turn when it meets the stairs. Sapey sofas, table, and carpet, an *Orgone* table by Marc Newson, and *IC Lights* by Michael Anastassiades for Flos.

AD N° 128, October 2017

Madrid

Fashion designer Agatha Ruiz de la Prada refreshed her penthouse by simply using paint in a very daring way, with white and yellow stripes, plus explosive combinations of fuchsia, green, and blue. Large-format contemporary art resonates with colorful furniture in unexpected shapes. A painting by Julian Opie and a monolith by Guy de Rougemont, a *Getsuen* armchair by Masanori Umeda for Edra, and a *Screw* coffee table by Eero Aarnio for Adelta.

Barcelona

Interior designer Marcos Catalán looked to Alvar Aalto's use of wood and light as inspiration for this family apartment. In the master bedroom, a Venetian mosaic floor acts as a foil for a wooden headboard, bench, bedside tables, and round table designed by Catalán and decorated with Lusesita ceramics, placed on an esparto rug. On the wall, oils by Maria Yelletisch from the Miquel Alzueta Gallery.

AD N°144, March 2019

Madrid

Interior stylist Jaime Lacasa worked with architect Emilio Sánchez to transform a turn-of-the-century building: green walls and aged wood set the tone for treasures accumulated through a lifetime of travel. In the living room, a Moroccan tile fireplace is surrounded by screens made with mirrors from India. Swedish chairs, Roger Capron's *Vallauris* ceramic table with a 1960s vase, and planters made from antique wooden barrels.

Madrid

Interior design studio Las 2 Mercedes was inspired by Old Europe for this 19th-century condominium. Woodwork, marble, and parquet flooring play counterpoint to *Ekstrem* armchairs by Terje Ekström, a hand-painted screen and linen sofas, both by the studio, and 17th-century Spanish chairs. On the mantel sits a painting by Hugo Fontela and a sculpture by Francisco Leiro, both from Galería Marlborough.

AD N° 138, September 2018

Sorzano, La Rioja

The Madrid-based design studio Casa Josephine turned an early 20th-century building into a country home filled with folk furniture and sculptural pieces with surrealistic details by Gae Aulenti, Roger Capron, and Kazuo Motozawa. In the second-floor lounge, Catalan armchairs from the 1950s keep company with a French oil painting and 19th-century Spanish, French, and Eastern European ceramics.

Madrid

Designer Patricia Bustos stepped away from her usual pop style to make this palatial apartment serene and calm.
A sofa by Bustos, a Dooq *Playing Games* table, 1950s armchairs by Claude Vassal, and a floor lamp by El 8. On the
oak sideboard, also designed by Bustos, a lamp and vases by HK Living and Ferm Living. Paintings by Kiko Perez,
from the Heinrich Ehrhardt gallery; curtains by Güell Lamadrid.

Barcelona

Interior designer Lázaro Rosa-Violán, the force behind many a trendy hotel and restaurant, lives in a cozy
neo-gothic *palau* in Barcelona's Eixample district. His cut-and-paste style is evident in the dining room,
with a 1960 Pierre Cardin floor lamp, the 1973 tapestry *Arbre Parella* by artist Josep Grau Garriga, and a
19th-century cabinet. At right, a baroque console and a 19th-century lamp. Chairs by Oscar Tusquets.

AD N°100, March 2015

Barcelona

Interior designer Jaime Beriestain faced down turning 50 by renovating his Barcelona apartment, giving it a fresh yet restrained and mature look. A Bulthaup kitchen with acid-treated brass, green marble countertop and wall. A table lamp by Louis Kalff, *Faun playing double flute* engraving by Picasso, vintage stools restored by Beriestain in Dedar's *Patchwork Black*.

AD N°147, June 2019

Madrid

Businesswoman Marta Medina-Malo lives surrounded by marble columns and frescoes in her 19th-century home, where her passion for Spanish folklore is evident. Past meets present in the living room: original *Tulip* tables by Saarinen and the *Wiggle Side Chair* by Frank O. Gehry for Vitra dialogue with two *Malabo* sofas in gold velvet. Photograph by Mayte Vieta, from the Travesía Cuatro gallery.

AD
CHINA

A cultural identity
infused with
contemporary poetry

Compiling 30 pages from 105 issues since *AD* China's first launch was a challenge simply because we had too many beautiful choices. The final cut is world-class quality: 20 rooms from 20 different homes, integrated into a very poetic flow. Transcending the typical Chinese style as stereotyped from a Western perspective, the big picture these engaging images present is one of aesthetics rooted in Chinese culture and philosophy. One might be tempted to compare it to a cup of Chinese tea—elegant, gentle, and with a fragrant sense of coziness.

We are delighted to serve our readers this cup of "tea" with an authentic Chinese aroma— but where, exactly, is the Chinese essence in each of these 20 homes? It might be embodied by a rustic pebble, a piece of vintage furniture, a work of Chinese calligraphy...or even expressed by a teacup lid casually left on the table.

The homeowners behind these scenes come from all walks of life. Some have traveled the world extensively; some are Westerners who have settled in China; some are artists and designers who remodel living spaces on their own; and some value the power of design and invite professionals, whether Chinese or Western, to transform their homes. The collaboration between Chinese homeowners and Western designers can be a stimulating yet beneficial two-way learning process that dovetails different cultures while fostering patience and perseverance. Especially for Chinese homeowners, learning to appreciate design from a global perspective and maintaining their preferred lifestyle involves dedicated persistence and proactive communication. For example, a well-rounded kitchen design can look sleek and modern while being tailored to the practicality of Chinese stir-fry recipes as well as people's preference for gathering at a round dining table. On the other hand, design innovations such as electric tea tables specially created to accommodate the complete tea ritual enhance the Chinese lifestyle by infusing urban hustle and bustle with poetic rhythms.

We are seeing increased diversity within the new generation of Chinese—they master foreign languages, embrace distinct lifestyles, and have acquired a comprehensive understanding of art and design. However, as they widen their perspectives and stretch their minds, they more firmly and confidently adhere to their Chinese identity, and take it further by assembling cultural traditions, environmental sustainability, digital revolutions, and the like into a balanced life. It is never easy to open one's doors to greet the curious. These 20 homes and their owners have greeted us and our readers with the fragrance of Chinese tea and ink...just as China's growing design market will greet international attention with its immense potential.

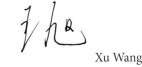

Xu Wang
Founding Editorial Director, AD China

Beijing

In this mansion, the Shanghai-based French designer Baptiste Bohu created a décor that blends the owners' dual French and Chinese cultures. Outside, the courtyard retains a richly layered Oriental feel, with a tea pavilion and paved pathway laid in "gold bricks," a feature widely used in ancient Chinese royal palaces, custom-made in the historic city of Suzhou.

AD N°97, May 2015

Beijing

The Lan Ying family's old three-story house plays up a love of wood with help from the Swedish architecture firm Claesson Koivisto Rune. On the first floor, an antique tearoom becomes a haven of peace, with a distinctive traditional imprint and modern wooden flooring. Ideal for enjoying a moment of solitude with a small teapot and a white magnolia porcelain cup.

Beijing

Baritone Tong Tiexin and
Lin Danshi, a restaurateur,
live in busy downtown Beijing.
Traces of Lin's artistic family—
calligraphy by her father, ink
paintings by her mother, and
pieces by her well-known sister,
Lin Tianmiao, and brother-in-
law, Wang Gongxin—fill an
open-plan living room that
functions as a painting atelier,
tearoom, and music hall,
with tall plants and easy sofas.

AD N°66, October 2016

Taipei

In the coastal town of Jinshan, Taiwan, the ceramists Cao Shimei and Xu Weibin converted a traditional house to reflect the concept of "imperfect perfection." Inside, discarded relics become a creative medium, and the house itself—their largest creation to date—likewise becomes a showcase for their art. Devoid of tiles, wallpaper, or paint, the interior plays up authentic glamour.

AD Special Issue, June 2014

Beijing

Despite an appreciation of Oriental aesthetics, this homeowner wanted to showcase her passion for contemporary Italian design. To bring it all together, she called on a specialist, Tao Jiang. In the main living room, a warm light gray is punctuated by armchairs, a floor lamp, and cushions in peacock blue. A painting by artist Qin Ai adds Eastern flair to an integrated space.

Beijing

Belgian national Juan van Wassenhove worked with his friends Lin Fan and Li Chow to restore the ancient Zhizhu Temple ("Temple of Wisdom"), a landmark more than 600 years old near the Forbidden City. The collaborative undertaking resulted in the prestigious Temple Hotel, but the architect also made himself at home on the grounds, in a renovated 1960s building where the focus is squarely on art.

AD Special Issue, June 2016

Dali

Chongqing-born designer Xie Ke spent three years deciphering the implicit language of a four-story building in Dali—and ultimately transformed it into his dream house. The spacious, bright kitchen/dining area also serves as a sitting room, with industrial-style frames and a selection of black furnishings. Refined details contribute to a sophisticated allure, and most of the furniture and objects are made of wood.

AD N°103, November 2019

Beijing

After visiting the country with his wife, the Venezuelan architect Antonio Ochoa Piccardo became part of the first wave of foreign architects working in China. Today, their Beijing home is filled with exquisitely crafted Chinese antiques from various periods. In the living room, an oil painting by Walter Margulis sits above the fireplace; in the foreground is a sculpture by artist Wang Shugang.

AD Special Issue, June 2016

Taipei

European furniture dealer and antiques collector Hsien Neng Lin lives in a reconverted 1950s-era tea factory in the mountainous suburb of Pinglin, outside Taipei. After nearly a decade of renovation, the building represents much more than a second residence: he sees it as a world of freedom and an ideal haven for communing with nature.

Hangzhou

Designer Chen Yaoguang converted a long-abandoned building into an American-style villa with a youthful spirit and a multifunctional layout. Its "imperfectly complete" design aesthetic marries in situ concrete walls with luxurious materials such as marble or granite. On the ground floor, a stylish private museum displays a collection of curiosities.

AD N°97, May 2019

Shanghai

This 1930s-era house was in an advanced state of neglect when the Franco-Chinese couple Sandrine Zerbib and Simon Wang came to its rescue with help from the Hong Kong–based designer Daniel Fintzi. A contractor experienced in renovating old houses carefully preserved its soul, while a décor of subtle elegance anchors it squarely in the present.

AD N°103, November 2019

Shanghai

When a young owner chose to make her home in a historic building full of classic charm, she asked designer Fan Minju of Maison to help preserve the apartment's original character. Restored classic art deco elements are accentuated by retro green walls and contemporary minimalist furniture—an exercise in eclecticism and inherent simplicity, with the grace of a 1930s lane house in Old Shanghai.

AD N°95, March 2019

Hangzhou

A native of Hangzhou, the curator, designer, and perfumer Siyu Chan grew up with the smell of fig trees in the family courtyard. When he acquired a three-story villa there, he planted new fig trees and opted for modern minimalism that shows a Greek inspiration, with organic archways, indoor gardens, antique wooden furniture from Morocco, and classic Nordic furniture set in a pure white space.

Shanghai

After architect Fernando Brando made a splash in China with his design for the Brazilian Pavilion at the Shanghai World Expo in 2010, he decided to stay on. His home in Sheshan is a modest, three-story detached building with an open living room and a seven-meter ceiling brightened by intense South American colors and Chinese elements, both traditional and modern.

AD N°94, February 2019

Beijing

Beijing artist Li Tao started with an empty construction for this three-story family home on the outskirts of town. Given the opportunity to play with elements and textures, he personally designed and furnished it, achieving balance without necessarily seeking it. On the top floor, a cozy "gathering nook" gives pride of place to humble materials and an artisanal spirit, accentuated by graphic orange-red tiles.

AD N°102, October 2019

Shanghai

In downtown Shanghai, this large family home has a startling open, luminous space, with a grand basement
and two floors above ground. dom.a, the design firm founded by husband-and-wife team Dominique Amblard
and Lin Wei, helped the young owners bring their dreams to life. Here, the master bedroom features a nested
concept, with unified, pure colors that create a serene, contemplative atmosphere.

AD N°86, June 2018

Beijing

This penthouse in the bustling downtown area of Beijing is owned by JinR, the founder and creator of Green T. House, a venue dedicated to authentic Chinese beauty, and her Australian husband, Robbie Gilchrist. Both nature lovers, the couple opted for earthy colors and muted shades, natural textures and simples lines. In the living room, deep sofas are draped in natural textiles and complemented by an organic cluster of ceramic pendant lights.

Beijing

Futuristic fantasy takes pride
of place in a high-rise in central
Beijing. Floor-to-ceiling windows
afford a magnificent view over
the megacity while, inside,
a 200-square-meter apartment
transformed by New York–based
designer Adam Sokol offers a
retreat for family, friends, and
colleagues. Nine independent
spaces are connected by 18
domes and archways, an exercise in continuity and fluidity.

AD N°92, December 2018

Beijing

When contemporary artist Zhang Xiaogang converted a three-story villa with a courtyard at the far edges of Beijing's Fourth Ring Road—near the 798 Art Zone and the Caochangdi ("grasslands") art district—he worked with architect Cheng Hui of WM Space Design to create a modern house with pure lines and earthy materials such as cement and wood, accentuated by his own distinctive works.

AD N°73, May 2017

Dali

An artist specialized in ink painting and calligraphy, Meng Zhong may look old-school, but his avant-garde ideas inform this collaboration with the emerging designer Zhao Yang. Inspired by the residence of the Sri Lankan architect Bawa, Zhao designed a series of functional rooms, punctuated by gardens and patios. In the living room, a large rubbing on the wall presides over a graceful space.

AD
MEXICO

Artisanal authenticity
to express the essence
of the Mexican soul

My homeland has the soul of an artisan. Mexico has a culture as rich as it is millenarian; it is built by revolutionary minds and artisanal hands. Today, we're seeing the emergence of an ambitious creative generation with a deep love and respect for its roots.

This book offers an ideal showcase for design that represents our culture and history, master craftsmen and creative geniuses, and to talk about spaces that define Mexico as a country that captivates and stirs the soul. A design philosophy that embraces essential, unpretentious luxury and proves that true elegance is rooted in simplicity.

Gabriel García Márquez once wrote that "things have a life of their own...it's all a matter of waking up their souls." The essence of the homes in this chapter resides in the details: in the quality of materials, in diversity of texture and pattern, in hand-sketches. They find their soul by bridging indoors and out, whether they are beach houses, forest retreats, country homes, or urban dwellings. In Ciudad de México, Valle de Bravo, Punta Mita, Colima, Valle de Guadalupe, Oaxaca, Hidalgo, Zihuatanejo, Tapalpa, Michoacán, Acapulco, and San Miguel de Allende, we discover design that invites us to dream.

Each of these interiors is a tribute to the new Mexican contemporary design. Modern, open, radiant, and cosmopolitan, some find balance in the connection between interior and exterior, while other, more rational compositions offer warmth through the fullness of natural light. Places designed to nourish the soul of their owners are the kind of spaces where we want to be: in these shelters, modernity, warmth, and generosity define the current "haute couture" aesthetics of Mexican design, which centers squarely on authenticity, handcraftsmanship, sophistication, and sociability.

The colors of Mexico are evident everywhere, eliciting strong emotions: shapes blend with natural surroundings, architecture and design unfold once you step inside. They are such intimate and calm scenarios, as they are open and generous spaces to treasure the most endearing moments of their inhabitants.

The leading creatives in these pages build the artisanal history of contemporary Mexico: they include Taller David Dana, Gloria Cortina, Covadonga Hernández, Bernardi + Peschard, PPAA (Pérez Palacios Arquitectos Asociados), Studio Panebianco, Kast Studio, CDM | Casas de México, MUMO Casa Creativa, Karen Collignon, Juan Collignon, Manolo Mestre, Legorreta Sepúlveda Arquitectos, ADI, ASHŌ, BAAQ', CCA, Zozaya Arquitectos, Elías Rizo, Karima Dipp, Daniel Cruz Maldonado, Ignacio Urquiza, Martiza Lara, and Vertebral. Each one of them draws an authentic, proactive, and colorful creative mosaic from their trenches that floods our soul with pride. Their visions and interpretations let us experience the pleasure and excitement of living in style and enjoying design at its best.

It is my great pleasure to share a variety of contemporary Mexican designs made for living life to its fullest—this selection of honest, human-scale homes truly represents the color and soul of our land.

María Alcocer Medina-Mora
Editor-in-Chief, AD *Mexico*

Ciudad de México

Studio Panebianco and Kast Studio, in collaboration with the artist Thierry Jeannot, created an atmosphere full of light, textures, and reflections. Chandeliers made of recycled PET plastic, by Jeannot, give this sanctuary a playful sophistication. The rainbow-style bench by Platalea Studio complements the offbeat lighting.

AD N°235, November 2019

Valle de Guadalupe, Baja California

The Bruma philosophy of harmonizing with nature and connecting with a structure's surroundings informed the design for the villas by Legorreta Sepúlveda Arquitectos and ADI (Gina Parlange and Mercedes Gutiérrez). Mexican furniture mixes with hanging lamps created by David Pompa and materials from the region, such as recycled wood, stone, and clay.

Ciudad de México

A judicious balance of materials, colors, and textures create an atmosphere that's cozy, friendly, and full of life. Anette Askenazi Shor, the founder of ASHŌ, was inspired by a mixture of mid-century classic style and contemporary elements to achieve an eclectic space. The use of blue demarcates the dining area, giving it a jaunty personality.

San Miguel de Allende, Guanajuato

At La Quinta, a weekend house designed by Pérez Palacios Arquitectos Asociados, the building offers
no views. To resolve the issue, the architects created three patios, each with a distinct character,
use, and intent. Different interpretations of scale and contrast, light and shadow, allowed the outdoor
spaces to become a complementary point of interest for each interior.

AD N°221, September 2018

Ciudad de México

Created by Taller David Dana, this apartment distills the essence of minimalism with a monochromatic palette, which gives it a timeless feel. Exposure and contrast are enhanced by the juxtaposition of elegant materials, such as marble, with more rudimentary ones, like concrete and steel, which create interest while preserving a uniform design scheme.

AD N°223, November 2018

Ciudad de México

One of the most important events of Design Week Mexico is Design House, where the most prominent local firms have an opportunity to give their creativity free rein. Here, a library by Covadonga Hernández, inspired by Sergio "Checo" Pérez, the Mexican Formula 1 driver. This contemporary space brims with revisited classic details enriched by an eclectic mix of shapes and materials.

Colima, Colima

This project's inspiration was to take the idea of a Mexican Pacific tropical paradise and create a home that evokes an endless vacation. A collaboration between Javier Dueñas from CDM | Casas de México and Kenya Rodríguez from MUMO Casa Creativa, Casa TM clusters within a circular patio that blurs the distinction between interior and exterior.

AD N°222, October 2018

Santa Elena
El Tule, Oaxaca

On the coast of Oaxaca, Casa Cal is located in the second tier of a development of six houses, which affords it an uninterrupted view over the ocean. José Alfonso Quiñones of the firm BAAQ' flipped the traditional layout, placing the social floor upstairs and private rooms downstairs in order to take full advantage of the vista.

AD N°225, January 2019

Punta Mita, Nayarit

Interior designer Karen Collignon always dreamed of creating her own house, so with the help of her father, Juan, and Manolo Mestre, she created Casa Koko, a villa with an egg-shaped palapa at the heart of the house and nine independent suites with sweeping ocean views. The furniture collection was inspired by Mexico and crafted in the spirit of timeless simplicity and gracious imperfection.

AD N°220, August 2018

Ciudad de México

The interiors of this residence, which dates to the 1990s, were totally reinvented by Gloria Cortina, who took a deep dive into the composition of each room and kept the focus on indigenous wood and collectibles. The new design scheme is highly conceptual: art, space, light, and shadow seem to merge, and a sense of atmosphere comes through in simple compositions and pure materials.

AD N°244, August 2020

Valle de Bravo, Estado de México

Located in an exclusive residential compound, this country home is striking for its stonework and the exceptional volumes from which all else flows. An interior design by Bernardi + Peschard Arquitectura combines the living and dining room areas into a unified space that opens onto terraces on either side, emphasizing an authentic connection with nature.

San Juan de Alima, Michoacán

The primary premise of this project was to maintain the visual and spatial relationship between the surrounding hills and the sea. The project, by Javier Dueñas from CDM I Casas de México and Kenya Rodriguez from MUMO Casa Creativa, is anchored by its imposing natural topography: thanks to a single-platform layout, interior merges with exterior.

AD N°239, May 2020

Acapulco, Guerrero

Daniel Cruz Maldonado approached a turnkey beach house for a large family like a blank canvas: raw textures, natural materials, and a limpid palette define this relaxed and peaceful getaway. With the exception of the Hans Wegner *Wishbone* chairs around the dining room table, all furniture was sourced from local design companies, among them Cotidiano, Adhoc, and Casa Mineral.

AD N°222, October 2018

San Miguel de Allende, Guanajuato

Conceived by PPA Pérez Palacios Arquitectos Asociados, this weekend house features several patios and high sliding glass windows that accentuate the interplay of light and reflection. The overall impression is one of purity and serenity. Intuitive, minimalistic design is the signature of the new, contemporary aesthetic in Mexican interiors.

AD N°221, September 2018

Ciudad de México

In designing a residential space where the owner, an artist, could also work and socialize, Covadonga Hernández of MarqCó conceived a peaceful indoor/outdoor–style terrace that also blurs the distinction between art installation and functional living space. This extension was constructed entirely in recyclable and sustainable materials.

Tapalpa, Jalisco

In this home, architect Elías Rizo, in collaboration with Karima Dipp, pays tribute to the lush Tapalpa forest. The interior décor is dictated by the natural environment, from the architectural process to the chromatic palette of ocher, sepia, and mineral tones. Locally sourced materials such as flagstone, steel, and parota wood show a commitment to authentic Mexican design.

AD N°216, April 2018

Tepeji del Río, Hidalgo

At Casa Moulat, Bernardo Quinzaños, Ignacio Urquiza, and Santiago Velez of CCA explore the duality of interior and exterior. A monolithic single-level house, it sits on a structural base of raw, gray concrete, and its interior spaces adapt to the surrounding topography. The project, a bellwether for the use of exposed concrete, integrates seamlessly with both the natural landscape and an adjacent artificial one—a golf course.

AD N°221, September 2018

Zihuatanejo, Guerrero

On an irregular trapezoidal plot on one of the highest hills in Zihuatanejo, Casa Z is accessed from higher ground. For Zozaya Arquitectos, the goal was to create a minimalist tropical home, with inviting spaces made using natural materials and local construction techniques so that guests may focus particularly on the panoramic view and exceptional climate.

Ciudad de México

The fledgling architecture firm Vertebral designed this project as "a house built for a garden."
Amid lush vegetation of palm trees, bamboo, and ferns that dissimulate property lines, a continuous
concrete shell rises up three levels from the foundations. Floating slabs of glass pivot outward,
effectively erasing the boundary between interior and exterior.

AD N°236, December 2019

AD
ITALY

Harmonizing styles and
eras: the transcendence
of Italian style

In modern décor, Italian style is not just an aesthetic canon: it is a state of mind. Its forefather, Gio Ponti (1891–1979), the architect, product designer, and interior designer, master of century-long creative ferment, wrote:

"I cherish the dream of a living, silent house that continually shapes itself to the versatility of our life, indeed fosters it with a hundred resources that we architects will teach, in order to enrich that life with light walls and furnishings.

A variable house, simultaneously full of memories, hopes, courage, and acceptances. A house 'to be lived in' when we have good fortune but also in times of sadness, with all it offers in steadfast faith and in an open, variable way, opening windows to allow the sun, the moon, and other heavenly bodies to enter along their course; all is in motion, those who descend and those who rise in the mystery of growth, and who knows what they will see. . . .

Art, architecture, and design should merge to create an environment that is capable of providing not so much comfort seen in its mechanical application of standards of measurement, which guarantee a minimum vital space, but instead the comfort necessary to also nurture the spirit of modern man, as we are taught by the Italian classical tradition."

Above all, he noted, "The Italian home is without complications, outside and inside; it welcomes furnishings and beautiful works of art, and requires order and space between them, not crowding or hodgepodge." Though radical at the time they were written in 1973, those words neatly capture the interiors illustrated in these pages. From Milan, Rome, Turin, Florence, and Naples to the provinces and remote locales like Pantelleria, these houses—variously the result of restoration, renovation, or new construction—stand out for their harmonious, cultured juxtaposition of age-old and contemporary, almost always elevated by a savvy composition of antiques and contemporary artwork, archaeological relics, classics of 20th-century design, and avant-garde experiments.

These interiors illustrate how the Italian approach to home décor is truly unique: there is an erudite play on styles and eras, inspirations and references, without slipping into fusion or hybridization, because its through line is about creating comparison and dichotomy, and reconciling differences through emotion. The process of eliciting convivial, comfortable, culturally stimulating spaces is a complex maneuver, entailing many seemingly dissonant factors.

Expressing the transcendence of Italian style—and highlighting and optimizing its many ingredients without missing its inherent irony—is the purpose of this chapter. These homes open a door to new perspectives on culture and tradition, as well as the present, while skirting the common (and relatively ubiquitous) pitfalls of false antiquity and modern ugliness. Likewise, the interior designers behind them invite the reader to attune to their sensibilities for understatement and theatrical flair, wisdom in composition, refinement, and good taste. The familiar embraces the new, ingenuity keeps company with intellectual refinement, and a counterpoint emerges between the enclosure and everything inside it. We must divine the clients' desires amid all this complexity and draw our own conclusions about the narratives in order to appreciate, as Ponti wrote, "the kinship between the very many things that are the expression, ornament, or instrument of our life, and of our fascinating home." *Benvenuto a casa.*

Ettore Mocchetti
Editor-in-Chief, AD *Italy*

Venice

The internationally renowned interior designer, set designer, and director Matteo Corvino reinvented an ancestral spirit for this elegant 16th-century mansion with an eclectic collection. The historic home is decorated with a composite of paintings and objects from Directoire to Empire, confidently arranged like an ornamental, refined literary itinerary.

AD N°458, November 2019

Naples

A superb landscape rich in chromatic shading seems poised to burst into an apartment designed by Giuliano Andrea dell'Uva with a tasteful and original reinterpretation of art deco. The city's colors are enhanced with contrasting hues, alternating with rigorous geometric patterns in black and white. Here, the furnishings are the protagonists.

AD N°440, March 2018

Matera

With an accent on essential refinement, a rationalist matrix, and discreet neoclassical touches, Andrea Truglio's stylistic signature sets the tone for this apartment. Classical works combine with others that define a new pop mythology, and a streamlined layout is enlivened by iconic designs, complementary brights, and signature ceramics.

Padua

In the historic center of the city, a duplex apartment in an 18th-century building looks onto an inner courtyard. Its refined, minimalist interior by Gionata Dal Pozzo and Mattia Cudiferro features an artful arrangement of design objects and furnishings set against the simple, quiet harmony of white walls and floors.

AD N°458, November 2019

Pantelleria

In a small Sicilian village, the Monastero residence exists in magical solitude. Built in the 1800s, the complex
is composed of *dammusi,* stables, and cisterns, nestled amidst prickly pear cacti. It was painstakingly renovated
by the architect Gabriella Giuntoli, who brought out the rural character of the spaces and enhanced them with
frescoes inspired by imagery from archaeological sites.

AD N°422, July–August 2016

Pantelleria

In the Monastero residence, the pleasures of revisiting the past invite a variety of inspirations. The dining room walls are decorated with encaustic work featuring black and green motifs borrowed from murals found in Pompeii. An original stylistic exercise, achieved by architect Gabriella Giuntoli, in which furnishings play a central role, with a harmonious blend of finely crafted pieces and family heirlooms.

Milan

On the fringes of Milan,
an Oriental atmosphere reigns
in a villa of delicate yet formal
clarity. An interior design by
Angelo Brignolli and Antonio
Feraboli of Studio Linea strikes
an ideal balance between a
Japanese sensibility and European rigor of shape, creating
an airy, relaxing style.

AD N°425, November 2016

Noto

Near Noto, Sicily, a mid-19th-century house recounts its history in a neoclassical manner: frescoed ceilings are offset by pale gray walls and columns in faux marble and granite, with meticulously curated furnishings and antiques chosen as an ode to proportions and symmetry.

AD N°446, October 2018

Rome

The kitchen is the heart of Fabio Massimo Bongianni's second-floor apartment behind the Piazza Navona. The prize-winning chef worked with Sara Lucci to put an accent on refined materials with an original personality, like the yellow onyx that frames a large fireplace. Every room has its own character, in relation to its paintings and sculptures.

Bologna

The apartment of the internationally renowned antiquarian Maurizio Nobile embodies the idea of artistic cross-pollination. Architect Enrico Bianchini set furnishings and artwork in a rarified atmosphere thanks to a skillful balance of lighting and pieces dating from different periods, creating an eclectic mix of eras and styles.

AD N°452, April 2019

Milan

Graphic interplays set the tone in Sonia Cocozza's apartment. The design journalist was deeply involved in the process, and the dynamic result features unusual geometries, recurring symmetry, and contrasting colors—a highly expressive visual language, elevated by the skillful use of subtle and vibrant color.

AD N°447, November 2018

Florence

In San Niccolò, on the city's left bank, Luigi Fragola Architects oversaw the restyling of a two-level home, combining a taste for the comforts of a country home with a refined, exclusive approach. Theatrical elegance and erudite references to art deco style blend with vivid contrasts, while vintage chandeliers and antique-finish mirrors engage in an imaginative dialogue with custom furnishings.

Turin

On the *piano nobile* of an 18th-century building, Paolo Genta Ternavasio created a dramatic ensemble for an apartment in which modern design finds a successful stylistic counterpoint in mirrors, stuccowork, and gilding. Spaces brimming with memories are layered with references to the 1970s—a striking combination.

AD N°450, February 2019

Tuscany

An old farmhouse facing the Crete Senesi, in Tuscany, takes its cues from the surrounding landscape with a nod to tradition. Authentic touches such as massive wooden beams and earthenware floors define ample, spacious rooms in a home steeped in nature-as-leitmotif. The *genius loci* is also present in photographs and design pieces, further enhancing context.

AD N°370, March 2012

Rome

In a two-story penthouse in the EUR district, theatrical staging pays tribute to the glory days of Italian design. A creative collaboration between Giulio Viganò-Corneli (for the architectural design) and Pier Paolo Rauco (for the interiors), this apartment owes its spectacular spirit to exceptional furnishings and marbles, as well as an impressive terrace-solarium with a sweeping view of the capital's skyline.

Florence

Else and Martin Berman chose
an apartment atop a late 19th-
century building overlooking
the Arno. Architect Valerio
Alecci reconfigured its interior
to encourage meditation, with
luminous, linear rooms to house
the owners' art collection while
accentuating the view.

AD N°425, November 2016

Padua

An antique barn in the countryside near Padua, transformed into an apartment with a modern spirit. The architect Filippo Coltro preserved its authentic rural character by using the original beams and exposed brick walls, encasing a barn with glass, and enhancing the rooms with works of pop-inspired art, designer pieces, and vintage movie posters.

AD N°439, February 2018

Brescia

Angelo Brignolli and Antonio Feraboli of Studio Linea redesigned this three-story neoclassical *palazzina* in a city in Lombardy, a project whose leitmotif is "elegant composure": pure lines and a delicate interplay of colors and materials let the French-inspired, slightly rusticated walls in Botticino stone, ivory, and gray play the leading role.

AD N°420, May 2016

Rome

Amid the age-old eucalyptus
and pine trees of Parco di Veio,
Marika Carniti Bollea created
a poetic, theatrical residence
for her children, devised like
a continuous game of echoes
and erudite reinterpretations
of artistic memories. Soft light
illuminates furniture in warm
hues, and hints of the past
create a dreamlike, cheerful
atmosphere inspired
by classical refinement.

AD N°402, November 2014

Naples

In Liberty Naples, an urban loft takes on a contemporary spirit based on an intentional contrast
with the stylistic tradition of the area. Filippo Arpaia and Luca Piscitelli focused on pure lines
to bring out the house's natural architectural order and created an interior narrative with "chapters"
based on different color palettes.

AD N°455, July–August 2019

Naples

A skilled treatment of volumes brings originality and architectural complexity to this *pied-à-terre* in central Naples. Renovated by Pasquale Capasso and Giuliano Andrea dell'Uva, it draws on original and detailed solutions to define various spaces, from dramatic staircases to two-story rooms. A precisely curated selection of furniture nods to Scandinavian classics.

Milan

Very contemporary furnishings
dialogue with a classical setting.
At the edge of Milan, Cinzia
Boffo Dal Pozzo came up with
a nimble synthesis for a 15th-
century villa, with décor that
uses contrast to dramatic effect.
Modern and contemporary
artworks set a decisive tone,
ranging from a trompe l'œil
fresco to a more austere,
linear aesthetic.

AD *Style Special Issue N°454,*
June 2019

AD
MIDDLE EAST

Embracing tradition
and modernity at
a cultural crossroads

How to sum up the decorative style of the Middle East? This sprawling mass of nations, tribes, and overlapping cultures has produced a rich blend of art, craft, and ways of living for millennia. For centuries, it has been romanticized and amalgamated in the collective conscious of the Western world, the exotic vignettes of Arabesque painting enhancing the fantasy. If I must be reductive (and I, too, am a Westerner, having moved from London to Dubai in 2017 to edit *AD Middle East*), then I would suggest that there is a tension between tradition (both real and idealized) and the aspiration to embrace modernity—gleaming glass-and-steel skyscrapers, contemporary villas overlooking the Gulf, and, most importantly, homes that embrace their setting and tread lightly on the land by harnessing sustainable building techniques, both old and new. The most impressive homes manage to balance these contrasting impulses to find a middle way for the Middle East.

Of course, the Middle East is known for lavishly decorated homes (although I must stress the opposite is also true), and we have featured several noteworthy residences on the pages of the magazine. Munib Al Masri's home, Beit Felasteen (which translates as "House of Palestine") is particularly extraordinary. The inspirational businessman and philanthropist has truly embraced the spirit of hospitality for which the region is renowned at this magnificent property, where no visitor is turned away from the gates. Sitting proud on a hillside in Nablus surrounded by Israeli settlements, the house is filled with classical art and antiquities and acts as a cultural beacon of hope to all Palestinians.

We were also honored to be granted access to the resolutely contemporary—yet suitably spectacular—Riyadh residence of HRH Prince Khalid Al Saud, who, as a trained architect, was perfectly placed to create a well-designed home for himself. The finished property, with chic interiors by decorator Robyn Jensen, skillfully balances tradition with modernity (the metal mashrabiya panels in the soaring marble-clad entry hall are a case in point), which Prince Khalid attributes to his studies in Switzerland and England. "I wanted to bring some of the positive design values from different societies back to Saudi Arabia—primarily simplicity, but one that is steeped in elegance," he explained. He has most certainly achieved that in his own home.

The Middle East has long been a meeting point for the different cultures and ideas that marched along the Silk Road and flowed across rivers and seas. Riad Habiba, the Bulgari family's holiday retreat in Marrakesh, is a magical fusion of Islamic and Spanish style, inspired by centuries-old links between the two cultures. Paolo and Maite Bulgari wanted the house to feel authentically Moroccan, yet give a nod to Maite's Spanish heritage. Between the work of decorator Pablo Paniagua and the many artisans he commissioned, almost everything at Riad Habiba, which sits within the historic medina, surrounded by craft ateliers, is either antique or custom-made. Paniagua was also influenced by Spain's most important Islamic buildings, which date back to the 15th century, and Arabian courtyard living. The gardens feature traditional Moroccan plants, like orange and almond trees, rose bushes and mint, and flowers are cut daily to perfume the interior. It's a sylvan fantasia and the setting is utterly transportive. As Paniagua enthused: "The rooms are surrounded by courtyards, and everywhere there is the sound of birdsong, water trickling in the fountains, and the call to prayer coming from the mosques."

Talib Choudhry
Editor-in-Chief, AD *Middle East*

Nablus, Palestine

In the Rotunda of Munib Al Masri's spectacular home, an original statue of Hercules stands beneath a Dome of Mercy bearing the names of the four prophets. "I bought the statue because it fits my story for Beit Felasteen," says the businessman and philanthropist. "Hercules is viewed as the warrior who beat the East with his own hands, which serves as a fitting metaphor for willpower and courage."

AD N°19, March–April 2018

Marrakesh, Morocco

Decorator Pablo Paniagua was born in Malaga, Andalusia, a region at the heart of Spain's Moorish tradition.
He quickly understood what Maite and Paolo Bulgari were trying to achieve in their Marrakesh home.
"It was vital to the family that the house have real Moroccan soul, not a contrived atmosphere," he says.
Out of respect for Islamic culture, only Berber-inspired patterns were used for embellishment.

Nablus, Palestine

A staircase made of local limestone from the Cretaceous Period (around 149 million years old) leads to seven bedrooms on the second and third floors in Munib Al Masri's home. A self-made billionaire, Al Masri is often referred to as the "Godfather" or "Duke of Nablus." His home, which he began building with his son Rabih in 1998, is a replica of La Rotonda, Andrea Palladio's Renaissance villa just outside Vicenza in northern Italy.

Nablus, Palestine

The dining room in Munib Al Masri's home is called the Nazareth/Bethlehem room. Above the fireplace flanked by carvings of two winged women is a Saf woven silk carpet from the Ottoman era. A 17th-century rock crystal chandelier hangs above the dining table. In the basement below are the ruins of a 4th-century Byzantine monastery. Archaeologists from around the globe have come to visit the site.

AD N°19, March–April 2018

Marrakesh, Morocco

In the Bulgari home, a tranquil green pool is surrounded by fragrant citrus trees and gardens planted with traditional Moroccan plants, such as orange and almond trees, rose bushes and mint. Flowers are cut daily to perfume the interior. The traditional white marble fountain warbles gently. The ebonized cedar sofa was designed by the decorator, Pablo Paniagua, and the alcala lanterns are of typical Marrakesh style.

AD N°23, November–December 2018

Marrakesh, Morocco

It may give the impression of being ages old, but 12 years ago this Marrakesh riad was little more than a vacant plot of land. The entrance courtyard of Maite and Paolo Bulgari's riad is furnished with a 16th-century Spanish chest with velvet and bronze details and brass lamps designed by the decorator, Pablo Paniagua. The tiled floor design is Paniagua's interpretation of traditional Moroccan mosaics.

Marrakesh, Morocco

One of three living rooms in the Bulgari home, with naturally colored tadelakt plaster on the walls and a coffered cedarwood ceiling inspired by 17th-century Moroccan palaces. The latter was designed by architect Gustavo Paniagua, the brother of interior designer Pablo Paniagua. The sofa and velvet armchair are by the Spanish company Tapiceria Veroe. Cushions in Rubelli velvet add pops of color.

AD N°23,
November–December 2018

Marrakesh, Morocco

Ash-colored tadelakt walls create an intimate feel in the library of the Bulgari riad. The iron fireplace inspired by the architecture of Marrakesh is by Pablo Paniagua. On the wall hangs an antique silk Berber wedding panel, mounted on Jim Thompson silks and velvet from Rubelli. The rug is an antique Moroccan kilim. The ceiling in oleander stems, by Gustavo Paniagua, is inspired by Berber *tataoui* decoration.

AD N°23, November–December 2018

Marrakesh, Morocco

In the Bulgari home, a small area next to the kitchen is dedicated to preparing tea. Teapots and glasses are displayed in an ebonized cedarwood cabinet inspired by the ancient buildings of the Marrakesh medina, designed by Pablo Paniagua and crafted by local artisans. Linen-velvet stools, also designed by the decorator, were made in Spain. The lanterns are local antiques.

Marrakesh, Morocco

In the master bedroom of Maite and Paolo Bulgari's riad, a 19th-century Moroccan tapestry adorns the wall; the bed canopy in silver silk is by Jim Thompson, and the knitted textile by Watts of Westminster. A bed designed by the decorator, Pablo Paniagua, and made by Tapiceria Veroe is flanked by antique Syrian night tables and a 1940s curule-style seat in gilded bronze, with green linen upholstery by Loro Piana.

AD N°23, November–December 2018

Jeddah, Kingdom of Saudi Arabia

A dandelion mirror hangs in the hallway of interior designer Laura Nazir's home in Jeddah. "The pieces that really stand out the most in my home are the mirrors," she says. "This one is by my favorite furniture designer, Christopher Guy." The chair on the left is by Baker. Antique sconces and curios picked up during her travels add to the refined yet rustic feel.

Jeddah, Kingdom of Saudi Arabia

Interior designer Laura Nazir's house has a laid-back, beachside aesthetic (no doubt an ode to the neighboring Red Sea). "The inspiration behind the interior design comes from the things that I have collected over my years of traveling around the world," Nazir continues. "I'm eclectic when it comes to the pieces I introduce into my home, and most of my favorites I found at either antique stores or auction houses."

Riyadh, Kingdom of Saudi Arabia

In the dining area of the "man cave" at HRH Prince Khalid Al Saud's home, realized in collaboration with
Robyn Jensen, a custom kaori wood dining table by Riva1920 is surrounded by *Mara* dining chairs by
Leolux. The *Shantou* metallic wall covering by Ralph Lauren chimes with the artwork—*Molten Sunset*
by William Laga—and a bronze fox sculpture from Lamsat'HM, a store run by Prince Khalid's mother.

AD N°23, November–December 2018

Riyadh, Kingdom of Saudi Arabia

Prince Khalid enlisted the help of the American interior designer Robyn Jensen, whose "impeccable" work he had admired at the homes of family members. The formal sitting room is a symphony of grays, and tactile materials like suede, velvet, and silk add textural interest. Coffee tables in smoked glass and bronze nod to the 1970s while the soaring ceiling is fitted with a custom-made light in Murano glass.

Riyadh, Kingdom of Saudi Arabia

In the family room of HRH Prince Khalid Al Saud's home, designed by Robyn Jensen, custom sofas and chairs by Donghia create a smart yet comfortable look, and a pair of curved étagères by Koket enhance the glamorous effect. The chandelier and branch lighting installations in the marble feature wall are both by Serip, while the *Rita* dining chairs by Mobi are covered in *Hollywood/Wilshire White* fabric by Donghia.

AD N°23,
November–December 2018

Riyadh, Kingdom of Saudi Arabia

In the entrance hall of HRH Prince Khalid Al Saud's home, designed with the help of Robyn Jensen, the floating staircase is topped by a custom-made, geometric screen painted in a matte bronze finish. It offers a contemporary take on traditional mashrabiya screens found in Arab homes and is flanked by vertical slabs in coffee-colored Emperador marble. The *bas-relief* hand-carved oak cabinet is from Grifoni Home.

Riyadh, Kingdom of Saudi Arabia

"Robyn Jensen was able to articulate and elevate my own design sensibility and, in the end, create something stunning, which is more than I could have ever envisioned," says HRH Prince Khalid Al Saud. In the formal dining area, *Campiello* dining chairs from Donghia are covered in *Venier Pietra* Jacquard by Rubelli and teamed with the *Mesa* dining table and *Roca* commode (Clan Milano); the *Tamburo* pendant light is by Oasis.

Beirut, Lebanon

Canvases by the French painters—and friends—Pierre Soulages and André Marfaing hang side by side
in the grand salon of an elegantly remodeled apartment in Beirut, part of a grand turn-of-the-century
house built toward the end of the Ottoman empire. There are several other canvases by French mid-century
abstract painters, including Hans Hartung and Georges Mathieu.

AD N°27, June–July 2019

Beirut, Lebanon

The owner of this Beirut apartment has a varied collection of art and artifacts, ranging from ancient to mid-century and completely contemporary. The gray-walled grand salon has a *Crescent Moon* sofa by Andrée Putman and a custom carpet from Atelier Diurne Paris inspired by a Pierre Soulages painting. The head on the Glas Italia side table came from Palmyra and dates to the 1st century.

Beirut, Lebanon

At the back of this apartment is a more private area, with the master bedroom and bath, further bedrooms, and secondary diwan that acts as a study and TV room. In the master bedroom, the bed is flanked by *Hiroshima* lamps by Karen Chekerdjian. A lithograph by the Bahraini artist Jamal Abdulrahman hangs between the windows. Graphic rugs and throws give the room extra punch.

AD N°27, June–July 2019

Beirut, Lebanon

This elegant but quietly energetic interior has a languid charm. The palm-filled diwan overlooking the terrace is fitted with custom-made "floating" marble sofas. Built in 1900, the house is located in the exclusive Wadi Abu Jamil neighborhood in downtown Beirut (formerly home to Lebanon's Jewish community), where a block of old houses and gardens has been beautifully restored.

AD N°27, June–July 2019

Beirut, Lebanon

"I didn't want a typically Oriental interior because Lebanon is not just Oriental," says the owner of this apartment. "Our identity, our culture is mixed." In the grand salon, the pairing of an old Milanese cabinet with bone inlay depicting rural scenes and an ancient Iraqi serving dish is a perfect case in point. Many of the antiques are family heirlooms.

Credits

AD US

PAGE 12: photo François Halard, style Carlos Mota, text Mayer Rus
PAGE 14: photo Trevor Tondro, style Howard Christian, text Mitchell Owens
PAGE 15: photo Scott Frances, style Mieke ten Have, text Emily Evans Eerdmans
PAGE 16: photo Shade Degges, style Colin King, text Mark Rozzo
PAGE 18: photo François Dischinger, style Michael Reynolds, text Mayer Rus
PAGE 20: photo Michael Mundy, style Carolina Irving, text James Reginato
PAGE 21: photo Stephen Kent Johnson, style Michael Reynolds, text Mayer Rus
PAGE 22: photo Stephen Kent Johnson, style Colin King, text Mayer Rus
PAGES 24–25: photos Stephen Kent Johnson, style Michael Reynolds, text Mayer Rus
PAGE 26: photo Roger Davies, style Anita Sarsidi, text Mayer Rus
PAGE 28: photo Kris Tamburello, style Michael Reynolds, text Horacio Silva
PAGE 29: photo Anthony Cotsifas, style Michael Reynolds, text Mitchell Owens
PAGE 30: photo Douglas Friedman, style Anita Sarsidi, text Dan Shaw
PAGE 32: photo Douglas Friedman, style Michael Reynolds, text Mallery Roberts Morgan
PAGE 34: photo Trevor Tondro, style Stephen Pappas, text Dominic Bradbury
PAGE 35: photo Jason Schmidt, style Michael Reynolds, text Mayer Rus
PAGE 36: photo Oberto Gili, style Carolina Irving, text Kate Betts
PAGE 38: photo Stephen Kent Johnson, style Michael Reynolds, text Mayer Rus
PAGE 39: photo Douglas Friedman, style Lawren Howell, text Mayer Rus
PAGE 40: photo François Dischinger, style Michael Reynolds, text Jane Keltner de Valle
PAGE 42: photo Trevor Tondro, text Mayer Rus

AD GERMANY

PAGE 46: photo Elias Hassos, style Ralph Stieglitz, text Uta Seeburg
PAGES 48–49: photos Christoph Theurer, text Sally Fuls
PAGE 50: photo Noshe, style Ralph Stieglitz, text Simone Herrmann
PAGE 52: photo Hiepler, Brunier, style Stephan Meyer, text Eva Karcher
PAGE 53: photo Thomas Loof, style Stephan Meyer, text Joseph Giovanni
PAGE 54: photo Nikolas Koenig, text Silke Hohmann
PAGE 56: photo Wolfgang Stahr, style Thomas Rook, text Ulrich Clewing
PAGE 57: photo Elias Hassos, style Thomas Skroch, text Friederike Weißbach
PAGE 58: photo Douglas Friedman, style Ralph Stieglitz, text Ulrich Clewing
PAGE 60: photo Deimel & Wittmar, style Stephan Meyer, text Ralf Eibl
PAGE 61: photo Elias Hassos, style Ralph Stieglitz, text Uta Seeburg
PAGE 62: photo Andreas von Einsiedel, style Johanna Thornycroft, text Reinhard Krause
PAGE 64: photo Gregor Hohenberg, text Margit J. Mayer
PAGE 65: photo Elias Hassos, style Ralph Stieglitz, text Lilian Ingenkamp
PAGE 66: photo Noshe, style Thomas Rook, text Bettina Schneuer
PAGE 68: photo Douglas Friedman, style Ralph Stieglitz, text Karin Jaeger
PAGE 69: photo Hiepler, Brunier, text Ulrich Clewing
PAGE 70: photo Gregor Hohenberg, style Ralph Stieglitz, text Reinhard Krause
PAGES 72–73: photos Ingmar Kurth, style Thomas Skroch, text Ulrich Clewing
PAGE 74: photo Gregor Hohenberg, style Thomas Skroch, text Simone Herrmann

AD INDIA

PAGE 78: photo Ricardo Labougle, style Gustavo Peruyera, text Supriya Dravid
PAGE 79: photo Tom Parker, text Manju Sara Rajan
PAGE 80: photo Iwan Baan, text Tora Agarwala
PAGES 82–83: photos Philippe Garcia, text Catherine Ardouin
PAGE 84: photo Tom Parker, text Gauri Kelkar
PAGE 86: photo Fabien Charuau, text Simar Preet Kaur
PAGE 87: photo Ashish Sahi, text Gauri Kelkar
PAGE 88: photo Bharath Ramamrutham, text Leena Desai
PAGE 90: photo Ashish Sahi, text Sunil Sethi
PAGE 91: photo Simon Watson, text Sunil Sethi
PAGE 92: photo François Halard, style Carlos Mota, text Dana Thomas
PAGE 94: photo Iwan Baan
PAGE 95: photo Bjorn Wallander, text Sunil Sethi
PAGE 96: photo Tom Parker, text Manju Sara Rajan
PAGE 97: photo Bjorn Wallander, text Mozez Singh
PAGE 98: photo Bjorn Wallander, text Greg Foster
PAGE 100: photo Simon Watson, text Sunil Sethi
PAGE 101: photo Simon Watson, text Abhilasha Ojha
PAGE 102: photo Bjorn Wallander, text Gayatri Rangachari Shah
PAGE 104: photo Ashish Sahi, text Gayatri Rangachari Shah
PAGE 105: photo Bjorn Wallander, text Sunil Sethi

AD FRANCE

PAGES 108–109: photos François Halard
PAGE 110: photo François Coquerel, production & text Sophie Pinet with the assistance of Jennifer Pouillaude
PAGE 112: photo Matthieu Salvaing, production & text Cédric Saint André Perrin
PAGE 113: photo Vincent Leroux, style Valentina Pilia, text Sophie Pinet
PAGE 114: photo Olivier Amsellem, production & text Cédric Saint André Perrin

Credits

PAGE 116: photo Alexis Armanet,
production & text Cédric Saint André Perrin
PAGE 117: photo Julien Oppenheim,
production Thibaut Mathieu,
text Marion Bley
PAGE 118: photo Adrien Dirand,
text Marie Kalt
PAGES 120–121: photos Jérôme Galland,
production & text Marie Kalt
PAGE 122: photo Ambroise Tézenas,
production & text Cédric Saint André Perrin
PAGE 124: photo Vincent Leroux,
production & text Cédric Saint André Perrin
PAGE 125: photo Jacques Pépion
PAGE 126: photo Alexis Armanet
PAGE 128: photo Aurélien Chauvaud,
production & text Cédric Saint André Perrin
PAGE 129: photo Jean-François Jaussand,
text Laurence Mouillefarine
PAGES 130–131: photos Julien Oppenheim,
production Thibaut Mathieu,
text Renaud Legrand
PAGE 132: photo Ambroise Tézenas,
production & text Cédric Saint André Perrin
PAGES 134–135: photos Jérôme Galland,
production Marie Kalt,
text Laurence Mouillefarine
PAGE 136: photo Paul Lepreux, production
& text Cédric Saint André Perrin

AD RUSSIA

PAGE 140: photo Mikhail Stepanov,
style Natalia Onufreichuk,
text Anastasia Romashkevich
PAGE 142: photo Mikhail Loskutov,
text Julia Lusenkova
PAGE 144: photo Stephan Julliard,
text Julia Lusenkova
PAGE 145: photo Sergey Ananiev,
style Natalia Onufreichuk,
text Eugenia Mikulina
PAGE 146: photo Sergey Krasyuk,
style Natalia Onufreichuk,
text Julia Lusenkova
PAGE 148: photo Sergey Ananiev,
text Maria Kryzhanovskaya
PAGE 150: photo Sergey Ananiev,
text Anastasia Romashkevich
PAGE 151: photo Sergey Ananiev,
style Natalia Onufreichuk,
text Ekaterina Kruglikova
PAGE 152: photo Sergey Ananiev,
text Sergey Khodnev
PAGE 154: photo Sergey Ananiev,
style Natalia Onufreichuk,
text Olga Sorokina
PAGE 156: photo Sergey Krasyuk,
style Natalia Onufreichuk,
text Marina Yushkevich
PAGE 157: photo Sergey Krasyuk,
text Julia Lusenkova
PAGE 158: photo Stephan Julliard,
style Natalia Onufreichuk,
text Anastasia Romashkevich
PAGE 160: photo Polina Poludkina,
text Olga Sorokina
PAGE 162: photo Sergey Ananiev,
style Natalia Onufreichuk,
text Anastasia Romashkevich

PAGE 163: photo Sergey Ananiev,
style Natalia Onufreichuk,
text Maria Kryzhanovskaya
PAGE 164: photo Stephan Julliard,
style Natalia Onufreichuk,
text Maria Kryzhanovskaya
PAGE 165: photo Sergey Ananiev,
style Natalia Onufreichuk,
text Maria Kryzhanovskaya
PAGE 166: photo Mikhail Stepanov,
style Natalia Onufreichuk,
text Anastasia Romashkevich

AD SPAIN

PAGE 170: photo Pablo Zamora,
text Rocío Ley
PAGES 172–173: photos Ricardo Labougle,
text Toni Torrecillas
PAGE 174: photo Daniel Schäfer,
text Eduardo Merlo
PAGE 176: photo Antonio Terrón,
text Enric Pastor
PAGE 177: photo Ricardo Labougle,
text Itziar Narro
PAGE 178: photo Manolo Yllera,
text Toni Torrecillas
PAGE 180: photo Pablo Zamora,
style Pete Bermejo, text Isabel Margalejo
PAGE 181: photo Pablo Zamora,
style Patricia Ketelsen, text Rocío Ley
PAGE 182: photo Montse Garriga,
style Gaby Conde, text Rocío Ley
PAGE 184: photo Manolo Yllera,
text Montse Cuesta
PAGE 185: photo Ricardo Labougle,
text Itziar Narro
PAGE 186: photo Manolo Yllera,
style & text Patricia Ketelsen
PAGE 188: photo Montse Garriga,
text Isabel Margalejo
PAGE 189: photo Pablo Zamora,
style Pete Bermejo, text Toni Torrecillas
PAGE 190: photo Eugeni Pons,
style Patricia Ketelsen, text Itziar Narro
PAGE 191: photo Pablo Zamora,
style & text Pete Bermejo
PAGE 192: photo Manolo Yllera,
style Pete Bermejo, text Toni Torrecillas
PAGE 194: photo Ricardo Labougle,
text Toni Torrecillas
PAGE 195: photo Montse Garriga,
text Rocío Ley
PAGE 196: photo Pablo Zamora,
text Enric Pastor
PAGE 198: photo Manolo Yllera,
text Eduardo Infante
PAGE 199: photo Manolo Yllera,
style & text Amaya de Toledo

AD CHINA

PAGE 202: photo Jonathan Leijonhufvud,
style Pete Bermejo & Kevin Ma, text Xia Yan
PAGE 203: photo Jonathan Leijonhufvud,
style Pete Bermejo, text Xia Yan
PAGE 204: photo Manolo Yllera,
style Patricia Ketelsen & Jian Han,
text Simeng Chen
PAGE 206: photo Manolo Yllera,
style Patricia Ketelsen, text Deyi Jiang

Credits

Artworks

Acknowledgments

AD US

Amy Astley would like to thank David Sebbah, Alison Levasseur, Michael Shome, Natalie Do, Shax Riegler, Mayer Rus, Mitchell Owens, Sam Cochran, Jane Keltner de Valle, Hannah Martin, Diane Dragan, Nick Traverse, Elizabeth Fazzare, Carly Olson, and the staff at *AD,* with deep appreciation to Anna Wintour for her continued support of *AD,* and our profound gratitude to those who opened their doors to *AD* over the past century, along with the creative talents who conjured up these unforgettable spaces.

AD GERMANY

Special thanks to: Thomas Skroch, Inka Baron, Reinhard Krause, Samantha Taruvinga, and Iain Reynolds.
Oliver Jahn would like to thank the many great interior designers, architects, and creatives we have worked with over the years, as well as all the homeowners who have opened their doors to us and supported our magazine. Thanks also to the entire *Architectural Digest* Germany team; their talent, creativity, and incredible dedication have made *AD* Germany one of the most authoritative and innovative magazines in its field.

AD INDIA

Greg Foster would like to thank Komal Sharma, Chandni Mehta, Tyrel Rodricks, Sarang Gupta, Sunil Nayak, and the *AD* India team. Additional thanks to *AD* India founding editor Manju Sara Rajan and founding art director Ashish Sahi. The entire team would like to thank the community of architects, designers, homeowners, and contributors for making magic.

AD FRANCE

Marie Kalt would like to thank Charles Miers and the whole Rizzoli team for believing in this project, and the editors-in-chief of all nine editions of *AD* whose talent and enthusiasm made this book possible. Special thanks to the interior designers, architects, and photographers who have worked with the magazine over the last 20 years. Thanks also to everyone on the *AD* team whose talent and creativity have made the magazine an endless source of inspiration.

AD RUSSIA

Anastasia Romashkevich would like to thank the *AD* Russia team, Maria Kuznetsova (managing editor), Alena Cherepanova (photo editor), and Laura Mills (translator).

Acknowledgments

AD SPAIN

Enric Pastor would like to thank Alejandro Romero (art director), Isabel Margalejo (features editor), Elena Francés (photo editor), Cynthia Ajras (editorial assistant), Reyes Domínguez (photo and syndication director), Sandra Fernández (syndication), Eva Vergarachea (archive), and Rosana Vicente (production).

AD Spain would like to thank their amazing team of photographers, stylists, and writers who work along with the best interior designers, architects, and extremely hospitable homeowners. Together they manage to upholster and decorate in a brilliant way each page of the magazine.

AD CHINA

Special thanks to: Xu Wang (founding editorial director of *AD* China), Iris Kao (captions writer), Eva Peng (captions translator), Sharon Wang (opening text translator), and Sophie Fan (copy editor).

AD MEXICO

María Alcocer MM would like to thank the *AD* Mexico team: Katia Contreras, Loredana Matute, Priscila Casañas, and Fidel Núñez. All our gratitude to the architects, designers, photographers, and homeowners who opened up their amazing spaces for the last 20 years.

AD ITALY

Special thanks to: Giuseppe Pini, Federica Clari, Riccardo Bianchi, and Mario Gerosa.

Ettore Mocchetti would like to thank the interior designers Valerio Alecchi, Enrico Bianchini, Cinzia Boffo Dal Pozzo, Marika Carniti Bollea, Sonia Cocozza, Filippo Coltro, Matteo Corvino, Giuliano Andrea dell'Uva, Luigi Fragola, Paolo Genta di Ternavasio, Sara Lucci, Pier Paolo Rauco, Studio Linea, and Andrea Truglio for their participation in the creation of this volume and for their support of the magazine *Architectural Digest* Italy. He also thanks the entire *AD* team, whose talent and creativity have made *AD* Italy one of the most authoritative and successful magazines in its sector.

ARCHITECTURAL DIGEST
*THE MOST BEAUTIFUL ROOMS
IN THE WORLD*

First published in the United
States of America in 2020
by Rizzoli International
Publications, Inc.
300 Park Avenue South
New York, NY 10010
rizzoliusa.com

© 2020 ARCHITECTURAL
DIGEST

FOR *ARCHITECTURAL
DIGEST*

Editorial direction:
Marie Kalt
Editorial coordination:
Pauline Langlois

Creative direction:
Thibaut Mathieu
Art direction:
Alice Mesguich
Iconographic research:
Shirley Doukhan
Sophia Bizounkad

Texts:
Amy Astley
Oliver Jahn
Greg Foster
Marie Kalt
Anastasia Romashkevich
Enric Pastor
Xu Wang
María Alcocer Medina-Mora
Ettore Mocchetti
Talib Choudhry

Editing:
Tina Isaac-Goizé
David Jaggard
Chantal Bloom

FOR RIZZOLI

Publisher:
Charles Miers
Editorial direction:
Catherine Bonifassi
Editor:
Victorine Lamothe
Production director:
Maria Pia Gramaglia
Managing editor:
Lynn Scrabis
Editorial coordination:
CASSI EDITION,
Vanessa Blondel

ISBN: 978-0-8478-6848-3
Library of Congress Control
Number: 2020934918
2020 2021 2022 2023 /
10 9 8 7 6 5 4 3 2 1
Printed in Italy

Visit us online:
Facebook.com/RizzoliNewYork
Twitter: *@Rizzoli_Books*
Instagram.com/RizzoliBooks
Pinterest.com/RizzoliBooks
Youtube.com/user/RizzoliNY
Issuu.com/Rizzoli